AF327440

the **FLAG**

edited by M. Lakshmanan

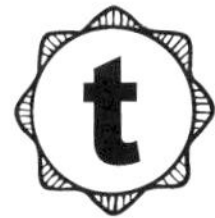

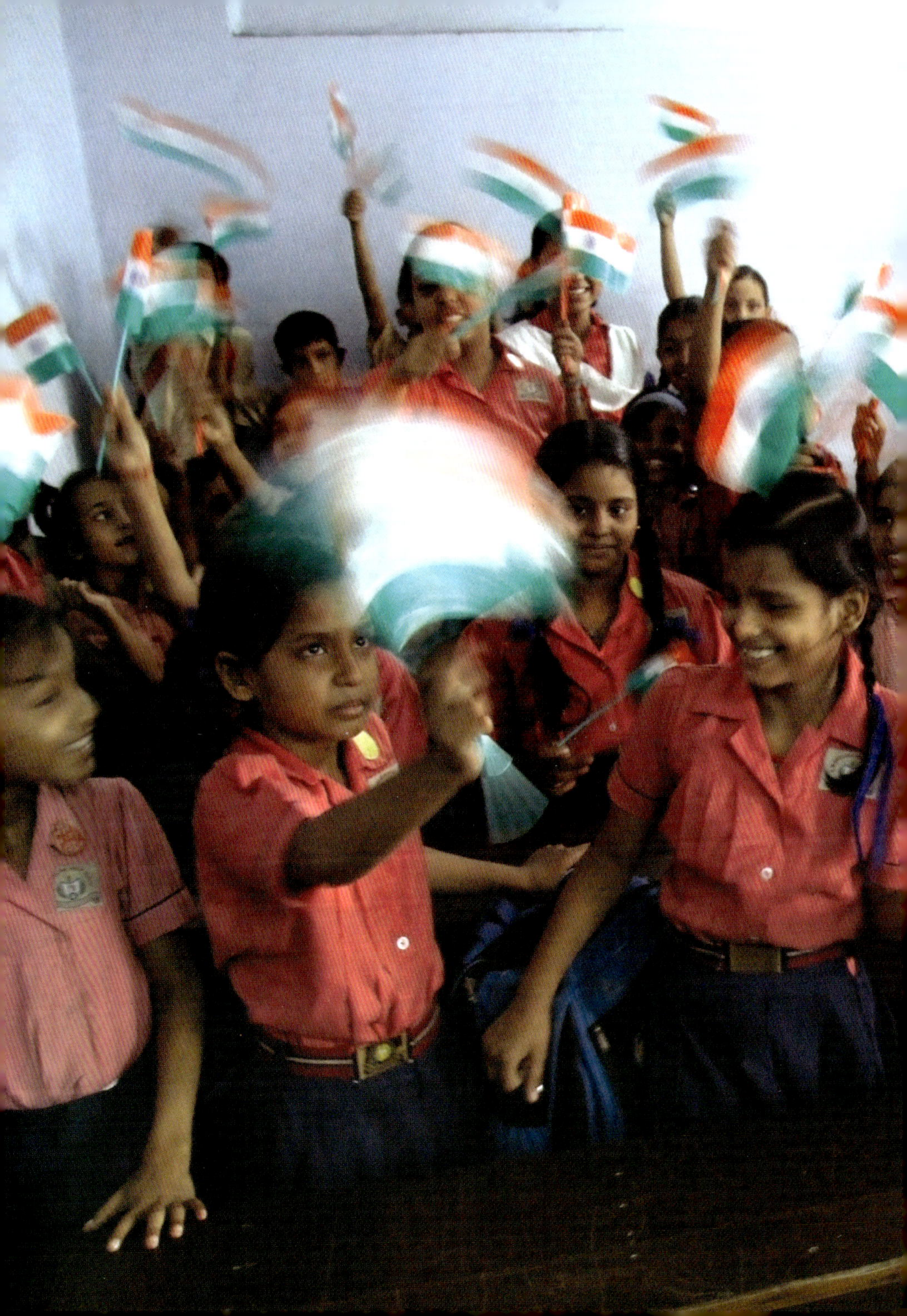

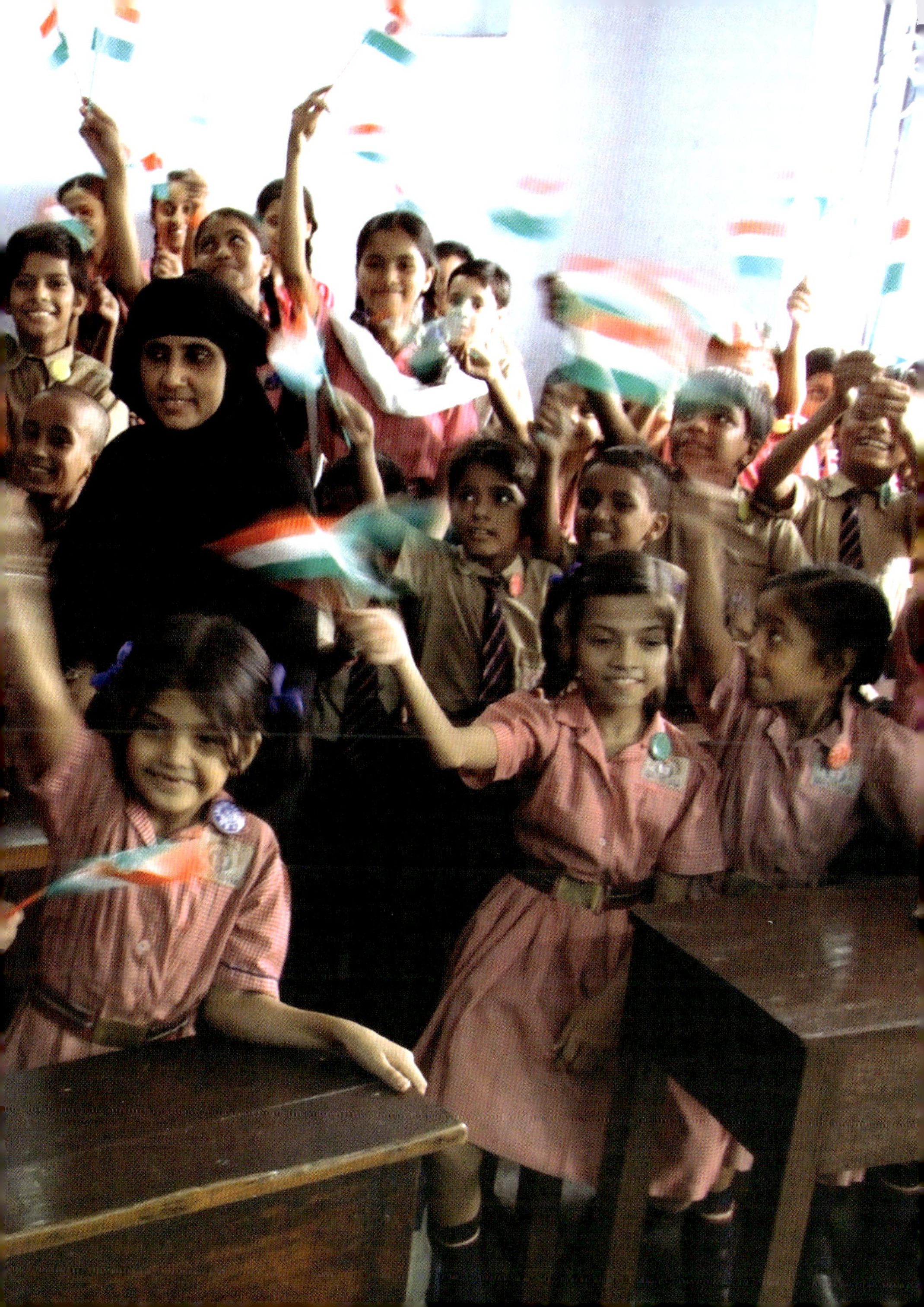

Every year, on the 15th of August – Independence Day – ragged street children dodge traffic, selling little paper flags to motorists on busy city intersections. It is an image that is hard to forget, a poignant moment in the celebratory story of citizenship and its meanings. It is also a moment that contains multiple signs – mixing, as it does, symbol, nationhood, patriotism, identity, commerce, poverty, desperation, neglect... And in the face of all this, a curious, ineffable, hope. This is the image that gave rise to the idea behind this book.

This first title in our *India Visual* series features the Indian tricolour in all its moments of pictorial glory and poignancy. As the visual syntax unfolds, it relates a complex and unusual tale, of everyday citizenship and patriotism. The moments which make up the life of the Indian flag are mixed – they are both grand and humble, carnivalesque and riotous, joyfully enabling and indescribably sad.

Press photographers from different parts of India are the book's narrators, bringing an unselfconscious and entirely refreshing vision to the story. Their rigour lies not so much in technical perfection as in a sure insider's grasp of the significant moment. We are witness to this moment in the most amazingly diverse settings. Brought together, they elaborate and complicate the book's argument in a persuasively democratic way – this sense of diversity is natural, neither forced nor cliched.

Each image in the book shows a private or public drama, involving the flag. Familiar sights from television and days of national celebration sit next to images that cause us to flinch – images where the flag is an object that is hawked by very poor and destitute citizens. Here it becomes the sign of an untenable exchange, involving poverty and identity, want and nationhood. These startling moments of visual disjunction cause us to pause, to look again at a page whose poetic beauty is belied by the still desperation of a flag-holding street child, eyes lit by a shy hope.

Other moments are more carnivalesque, when the tricolour becomes the badge of a happy and riotous companionship;

moments of comfortable joy which suggest an affirming – though unreflective – patriotic ardour. Then there is the aesthetics of the flag itself – festooning the streets, styling members of the body politic, and solemnizing nationalistic ritual in the most unexpectedly delightful ways.

It is this multifariousness that disallows sentimentality. The symbol of the flag is endlessly contingent: it is enabling, when it sits happily besides a seller of sweets, or is flamboyantly offered to the viewer by a pedlar of baubles. We marvel at the ubiquity of its presence across waterways and in the sky, in the humble rickshaw and the House of Parliament, and in the self-important hands of pompous military men. But if there is one constituency which makes us complicate the flag's promise of possibility, it is children. The yearning of the poor undernourished child with the flag is, sadly, in pitiful contrast to the excitement of middle class children enjoying the rituals of citizenship.

The Indian tricolour is probably one of the most familiar and cherished national objects in post-independent India. Its horizontal stripes invoke other such striped flags, memorably those that proclaimed revolution and democracy in nineteenth century Europe. But its colours – saffron, white, and green – represent a different history, of opposition to British rule and colonialism, and an affirmation of Indian national unity. Originally claimed for the cause of revolutionary nationalism, the Indian flag literally changed colour when Mahatma Gandhi showed keen interest in it. He initially imagined the tricolour as a symbol of unity and harmony between people of diverse faiths – but later on, explained the three colours through secular semantics: saffron for sacrifice, white for purity and green for hope.

The flag was never a static symbol. It was always held and waved in a spirit of pride and defiance. In British India it was a genuine symbol of sedition, rivalling the Gandhi cap. A sea of saffron, white and green often confronted colonial power with its own limits. On the other hand, a red-flag waving communist could and did call out to the nationalist flag-bearer to attend to other symbols and meanings.

When India became free of British rule, the flag affirmed the sovereign pride of a newly formed nation-state. In Nehru's memorable words, the flag was "concentrated history", a standard for freedom, not only for Indians but for oppressed people the world over. And so it came to mark India's distinctive place in the global concord of nations, both its unique identity and its readiness for fellowship. But the flag had to also mark conflict and national interest, paired with the very influential idea that a sovereign state is necessarily a militarily confident state. Unsurprisingly, in the crucial 1960s and into the 1970s, it was a silent yet eloquent sentinel, standing guard at India's borders, separating the patriot from the alien, the citizen from the refugee.

Today, the flag enjoys a double life. Raised and saluted ceremonially on national days, its use is bound by the strict Flag Code. Significantly, for those who brought the banner to life – for Gandhi and Nehru – the flag, however inviolate, came to life only in and through the actions of those who wielded it. Gandhi was as much concerned about the flag-bearer, and his or her capacity to embody the national spirit, as he was for the sanctity of the symbol. Nehru, while affirming the flag as an honoured symbol of the nation, also understood it to be an embodied compact, between the nation-state and the people. So the flag was as much of the people, as of the state.

It is this other life of the flag – lived out in the many and often unexpected ways of India's ordinary citizens – that is the subject of this book. In this sense, the flag is a powerful token of claim-making, and one that allows us to wear, claim, express and demonstrate the fantastic possibilities as well as the stifling limits of citizenship.

V. Geetha & Gita Wolf
Chennai 2010

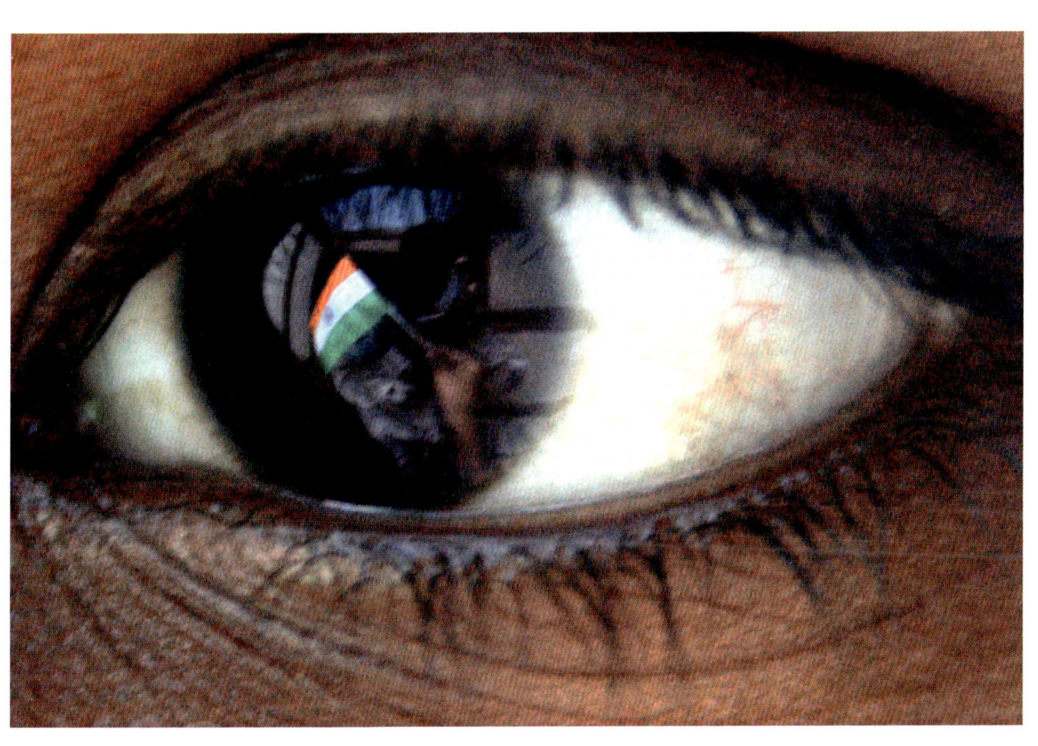

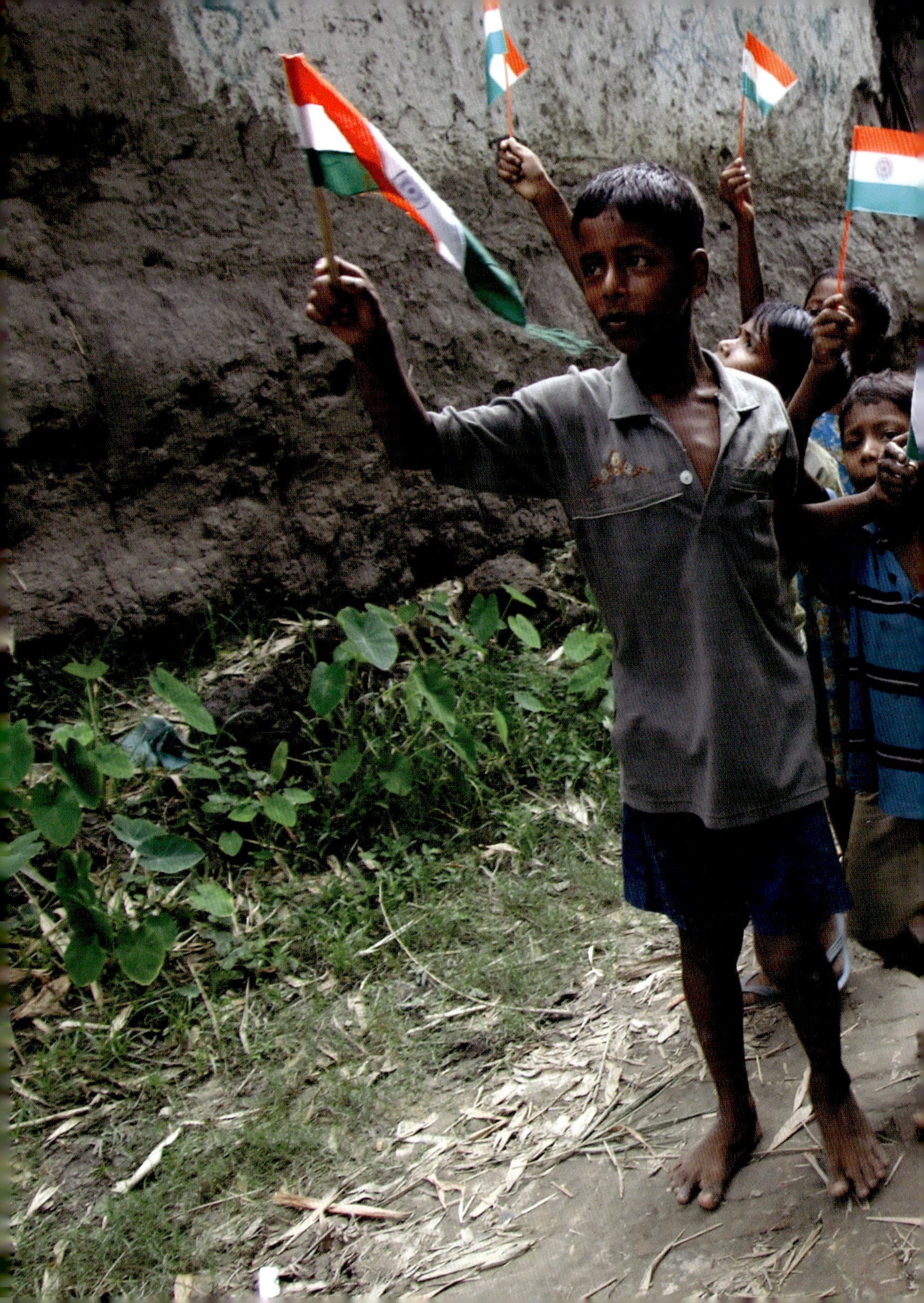

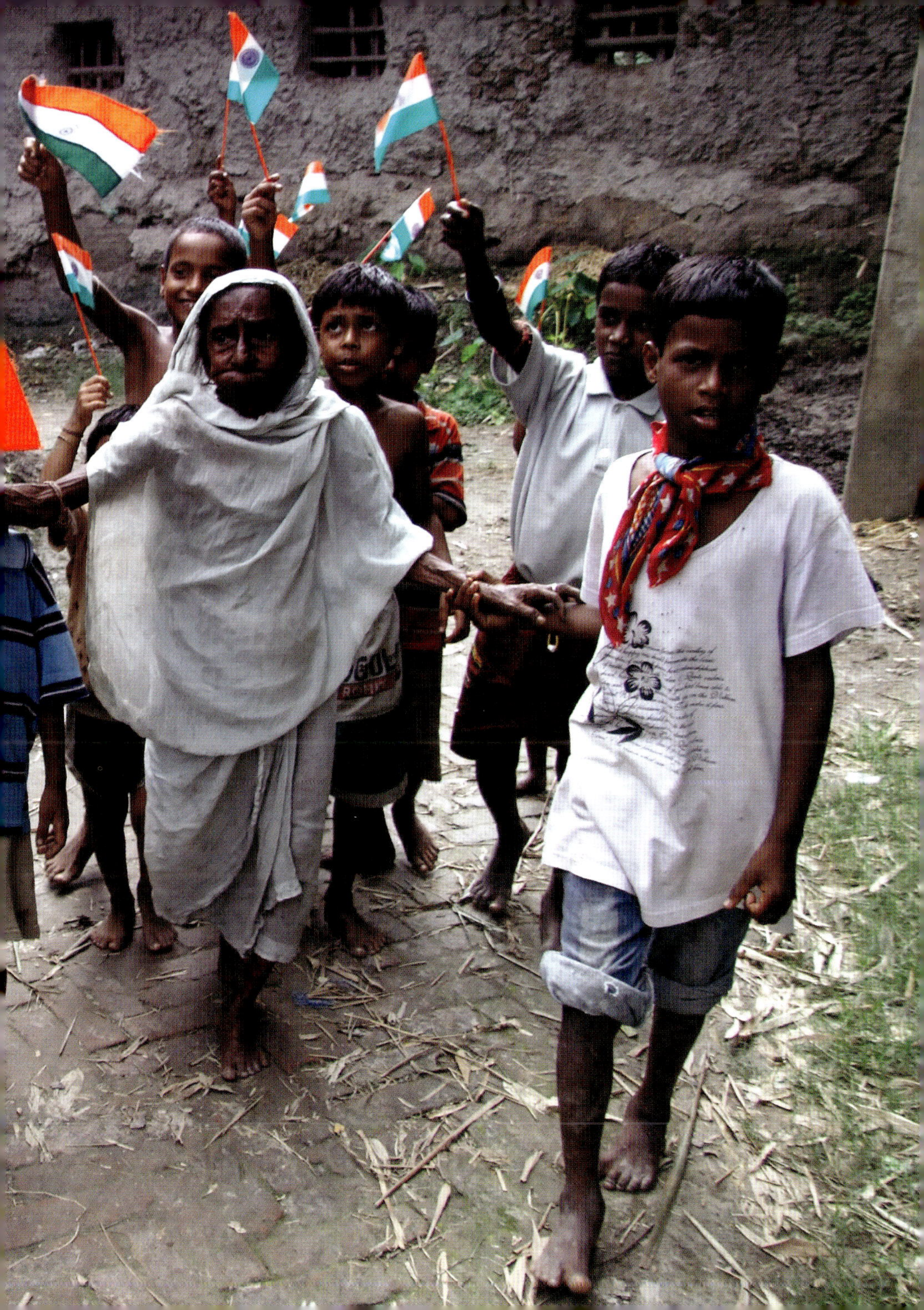

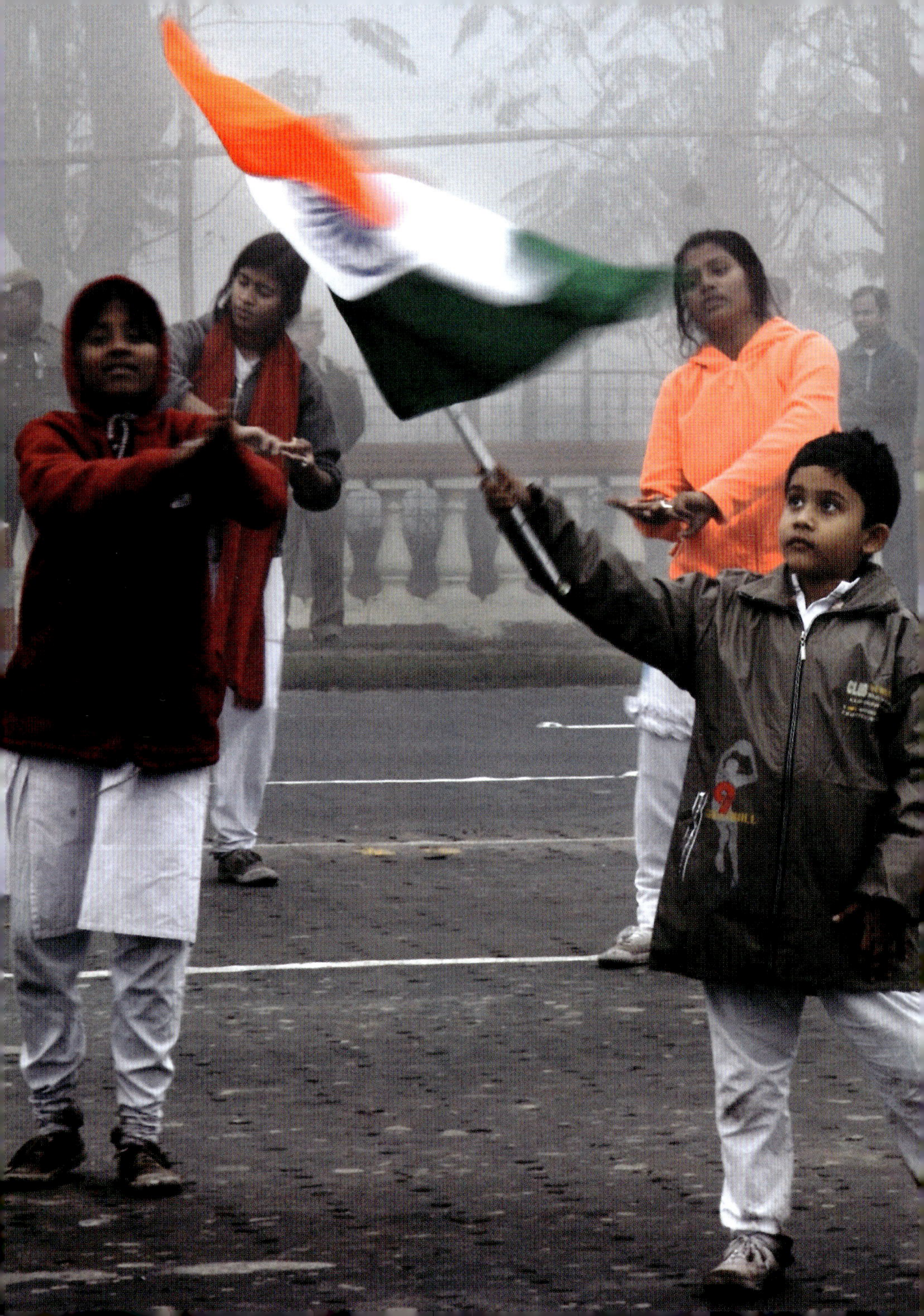

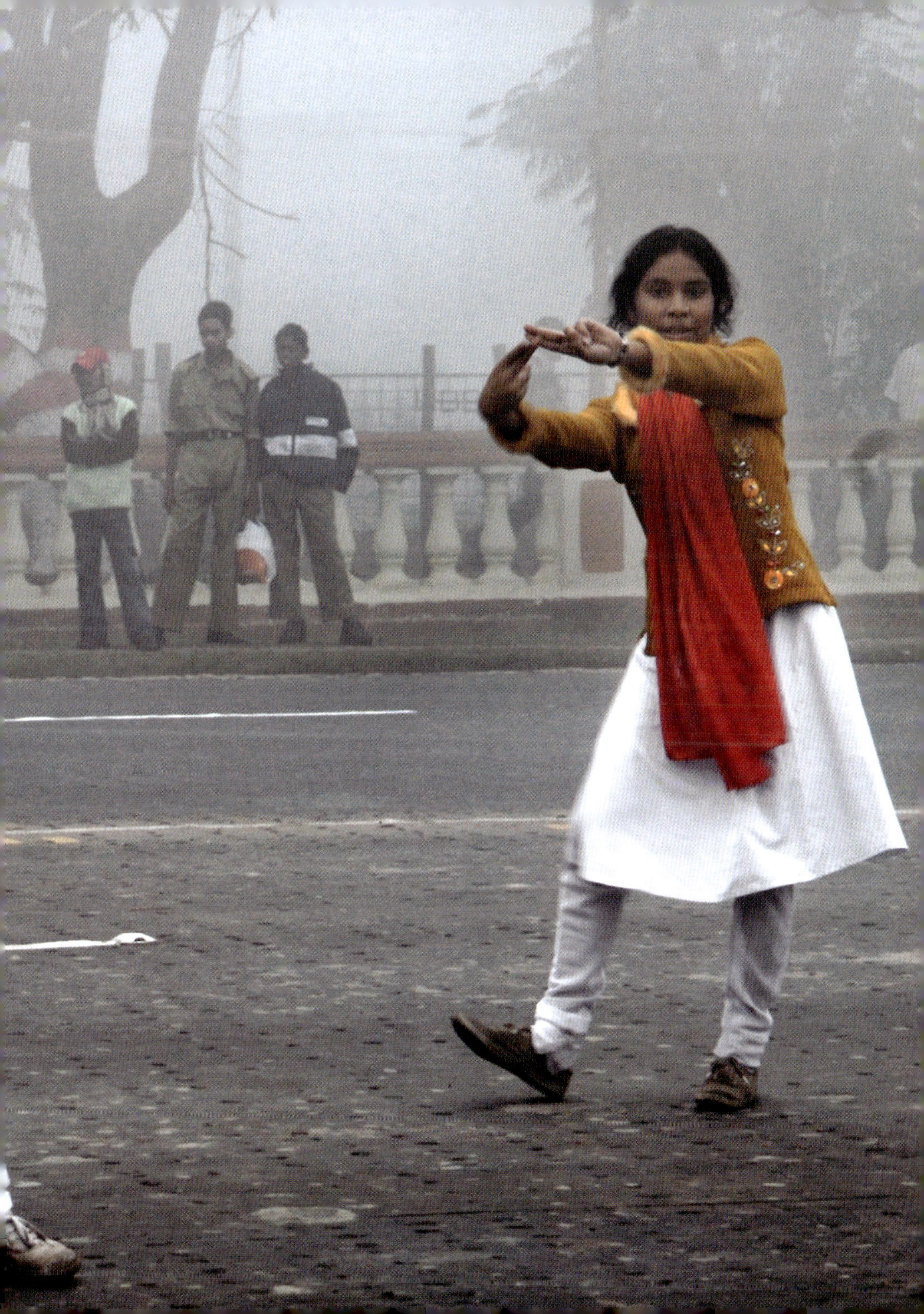

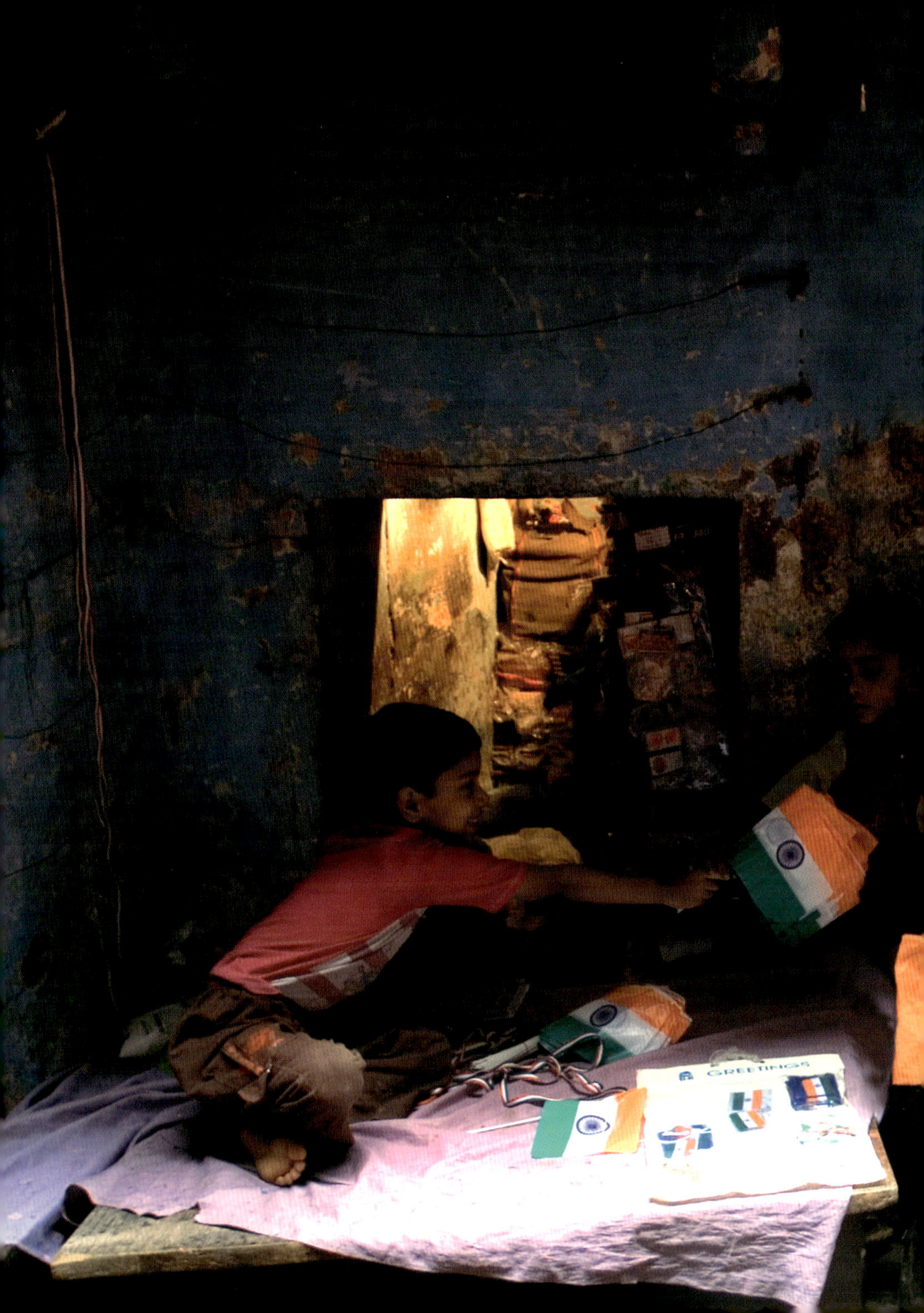

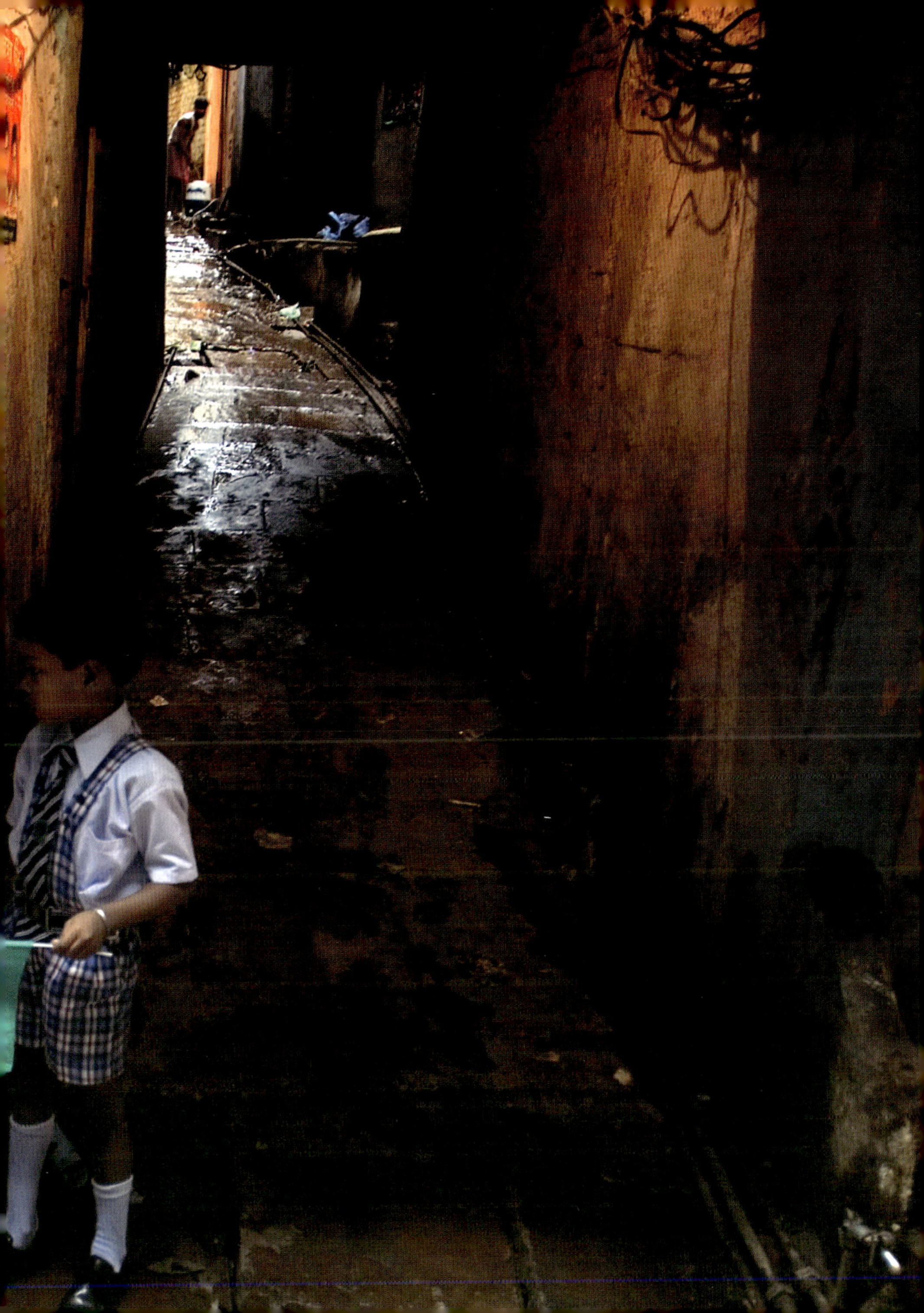

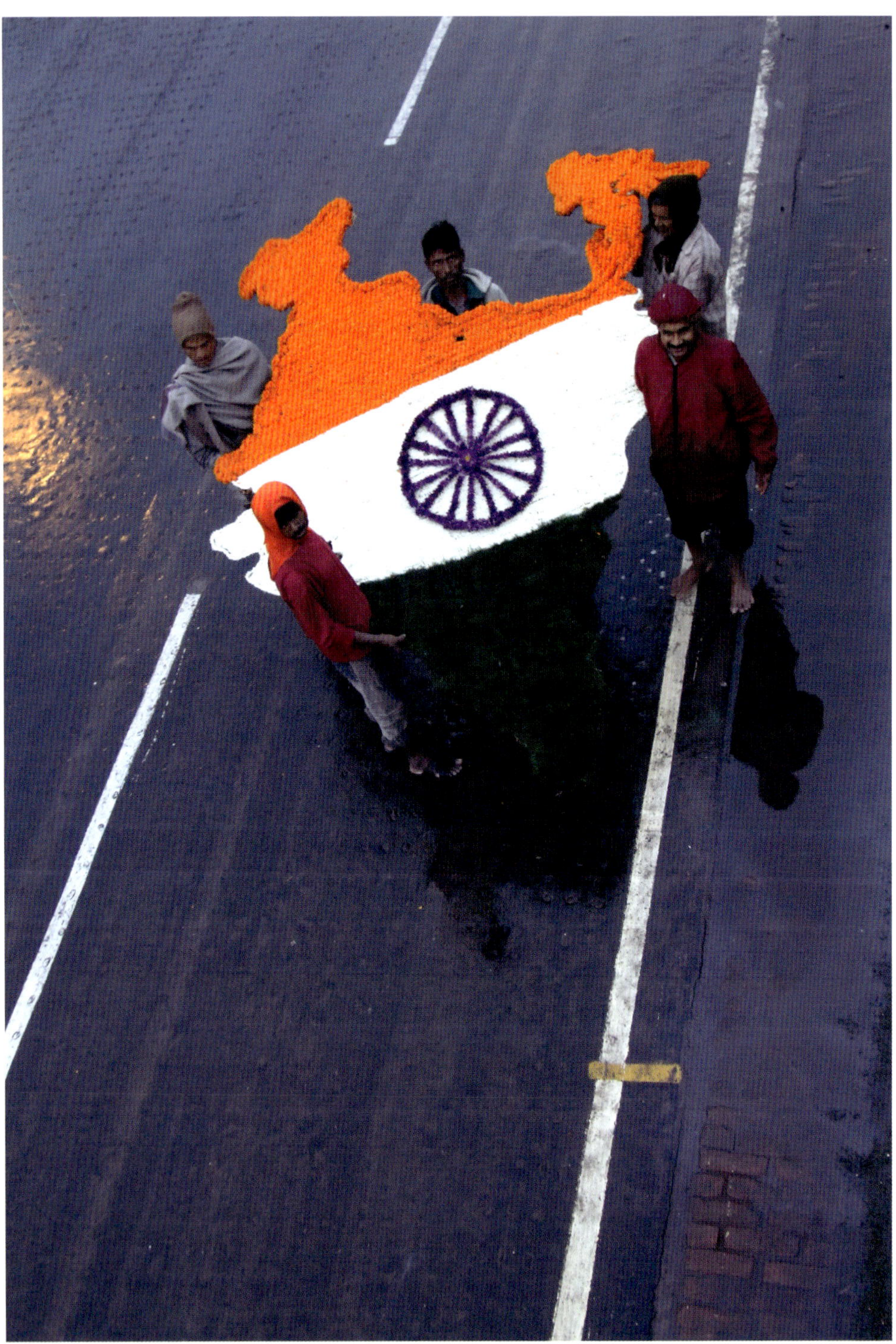

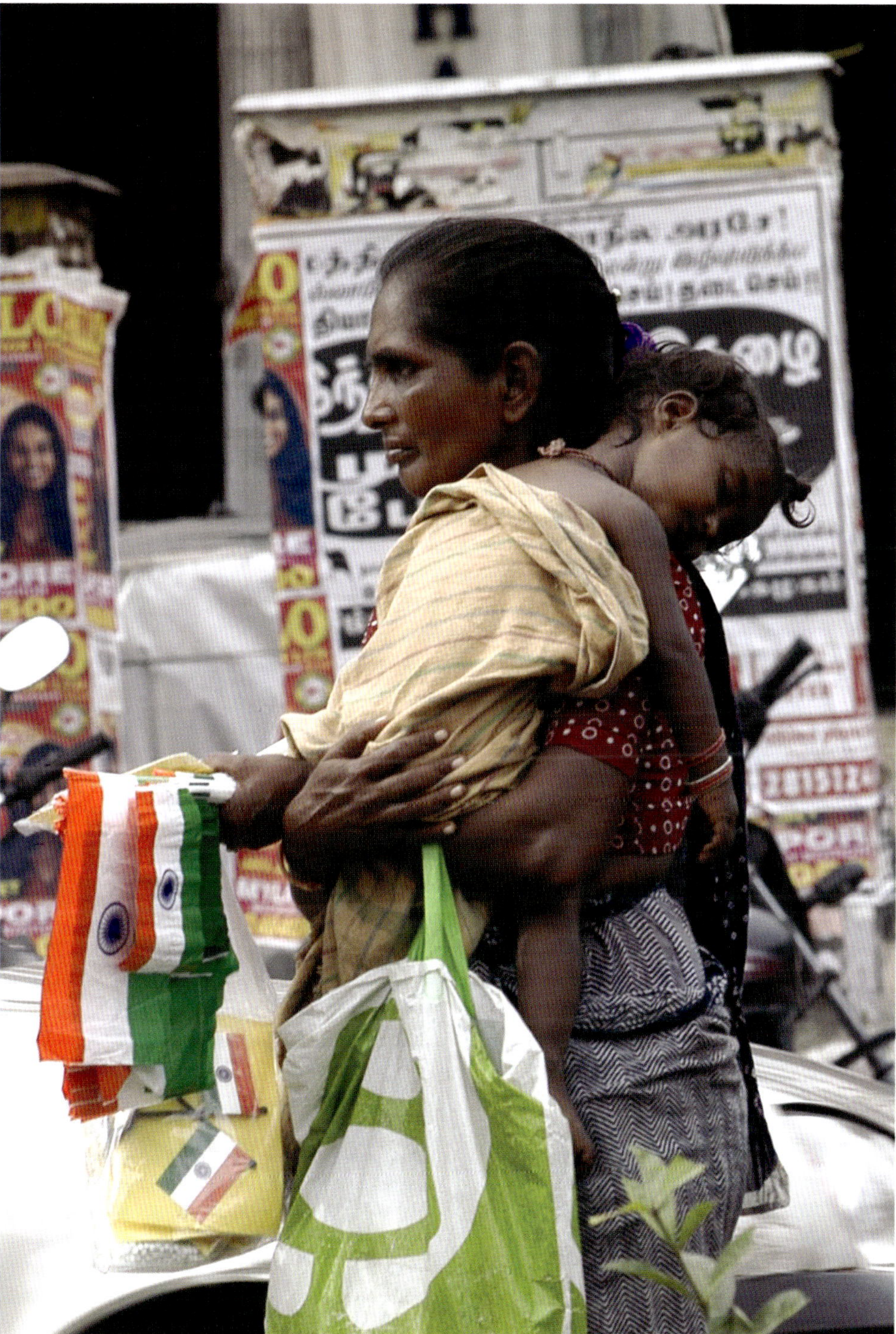

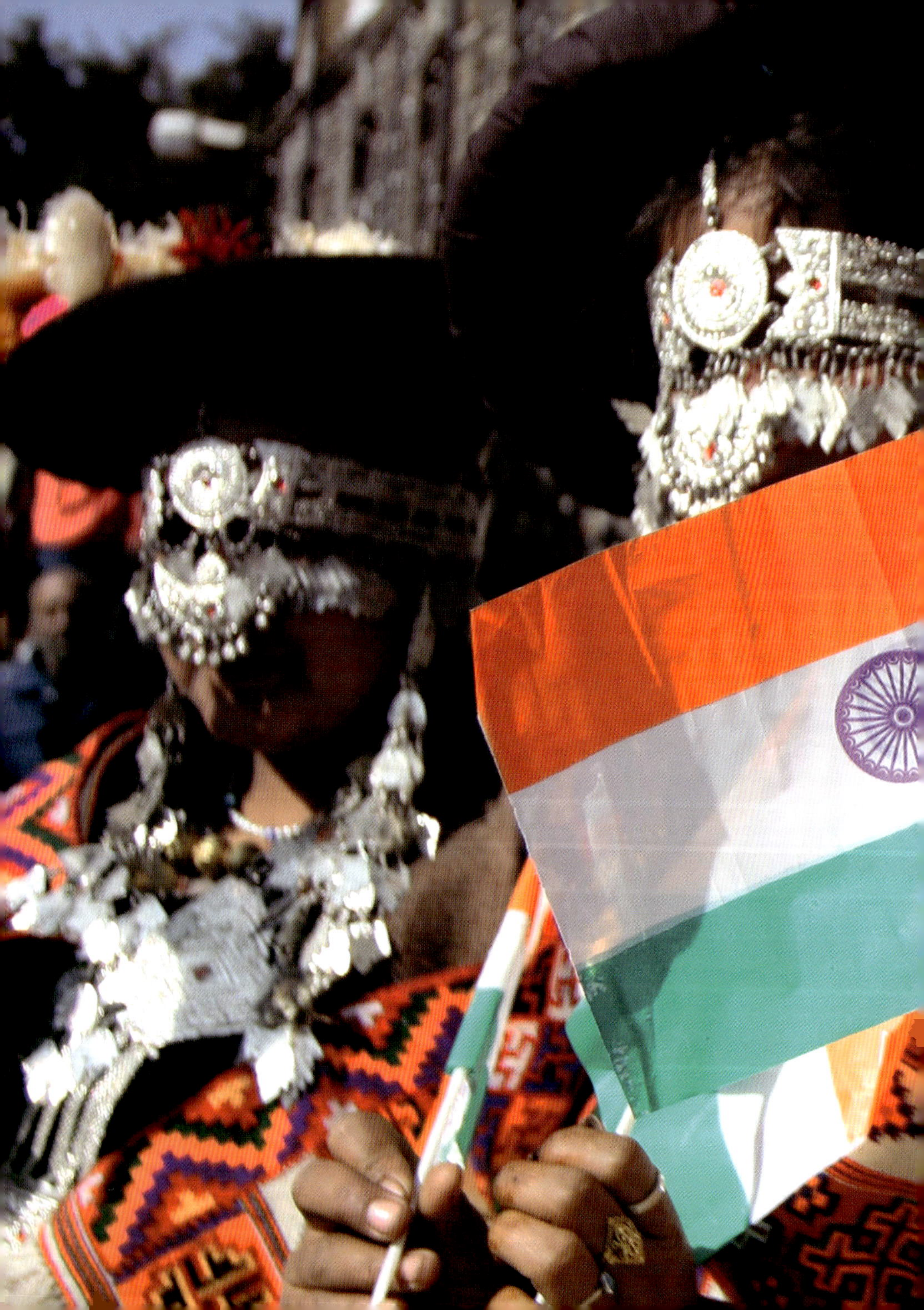

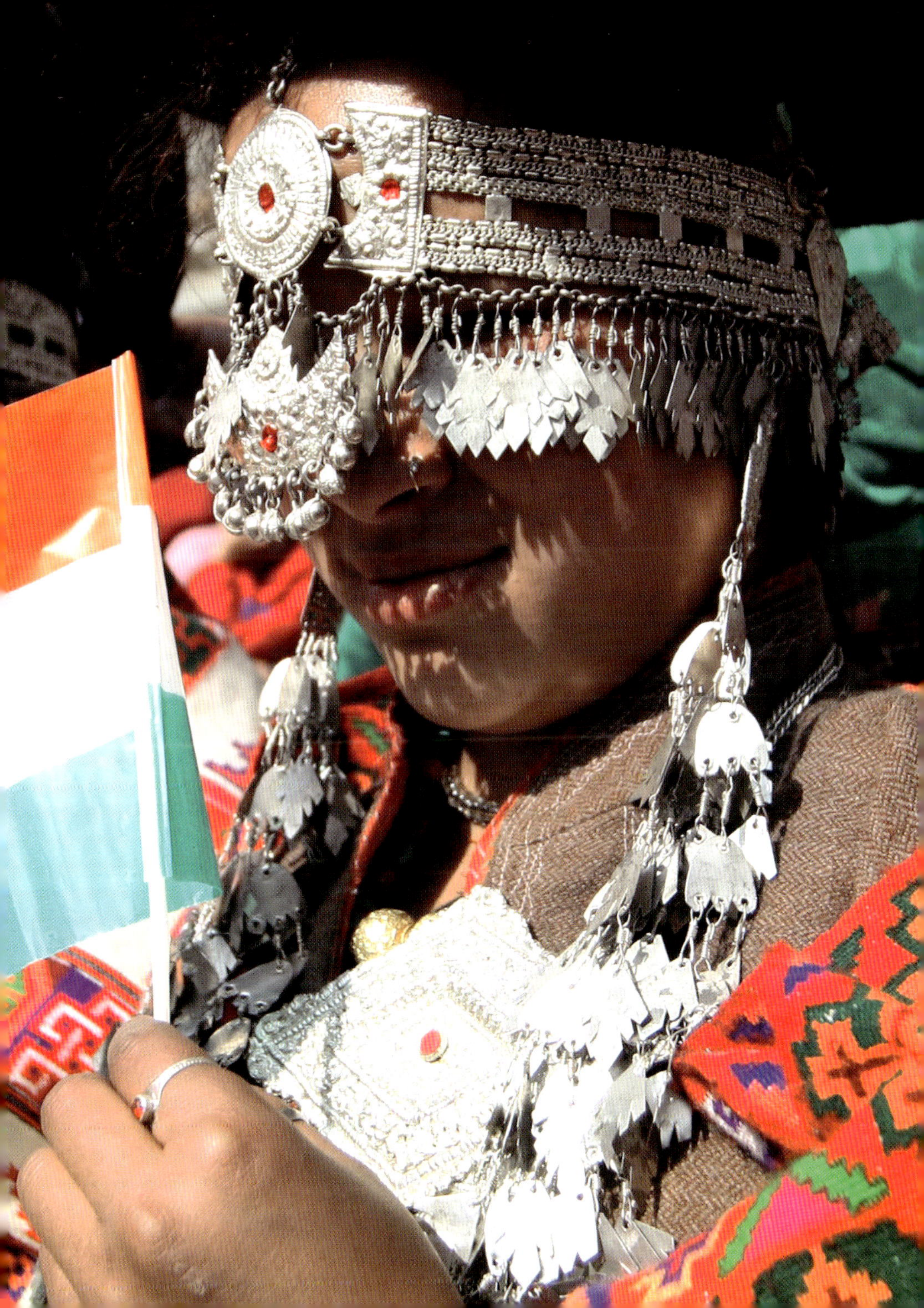

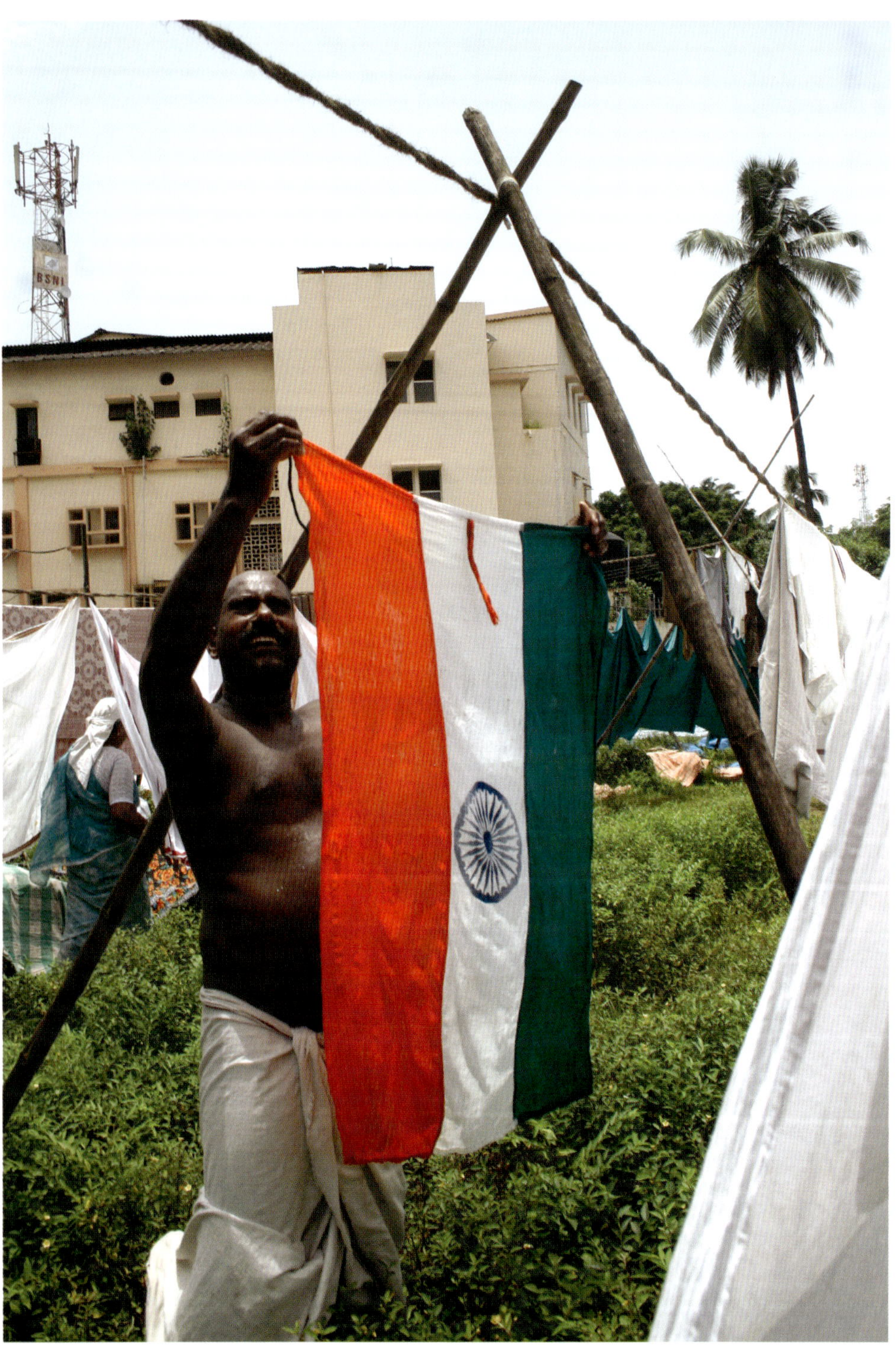

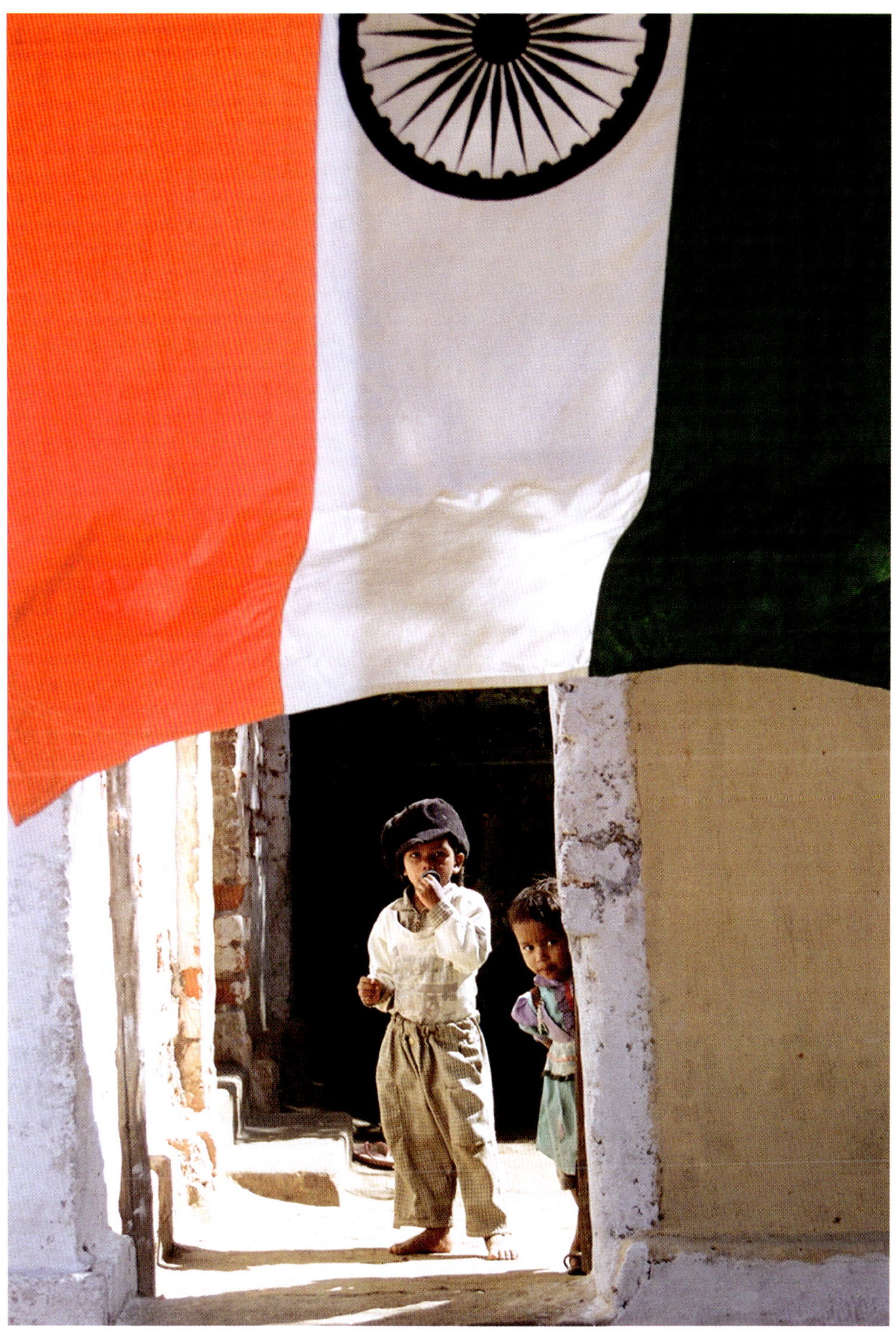

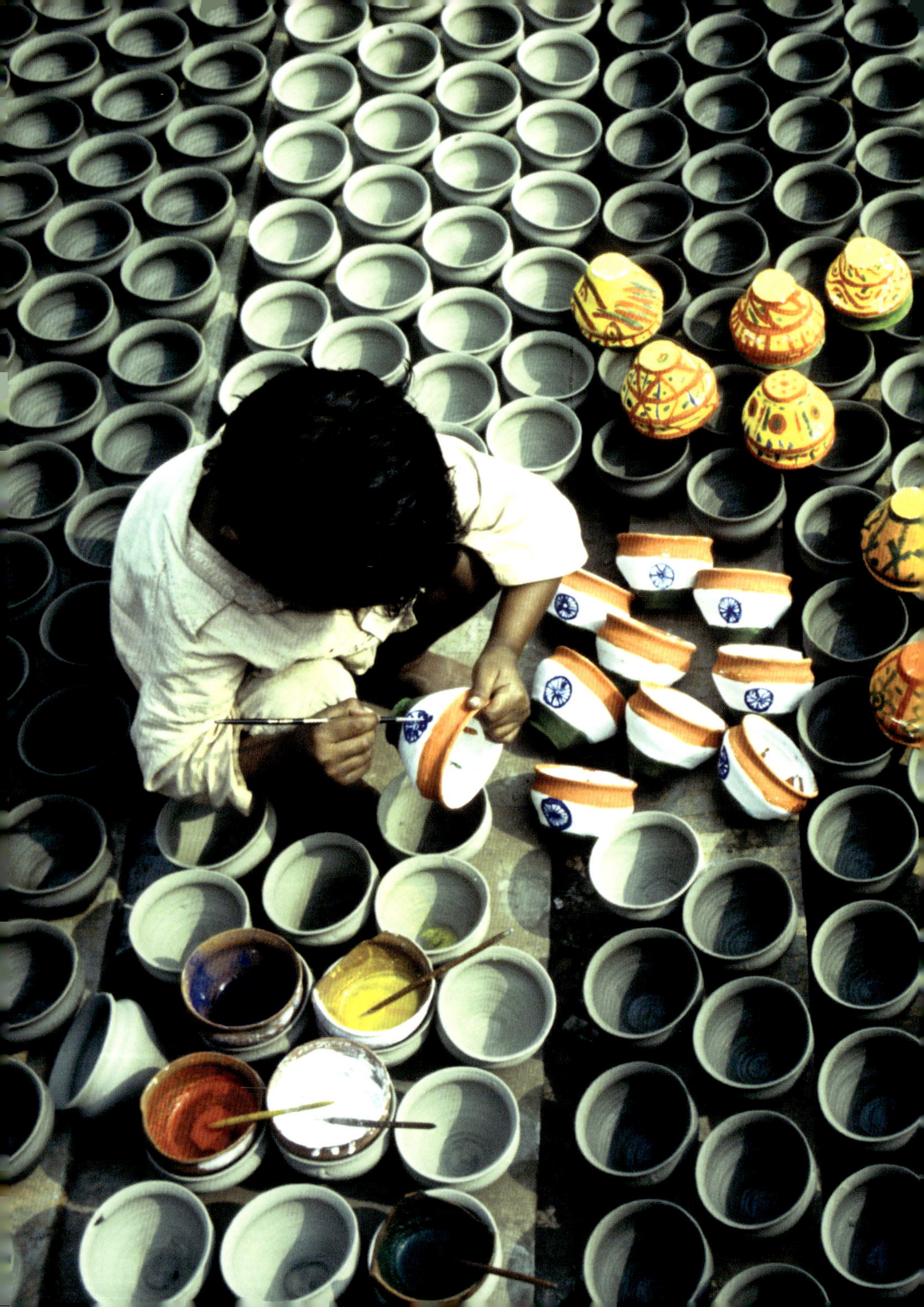

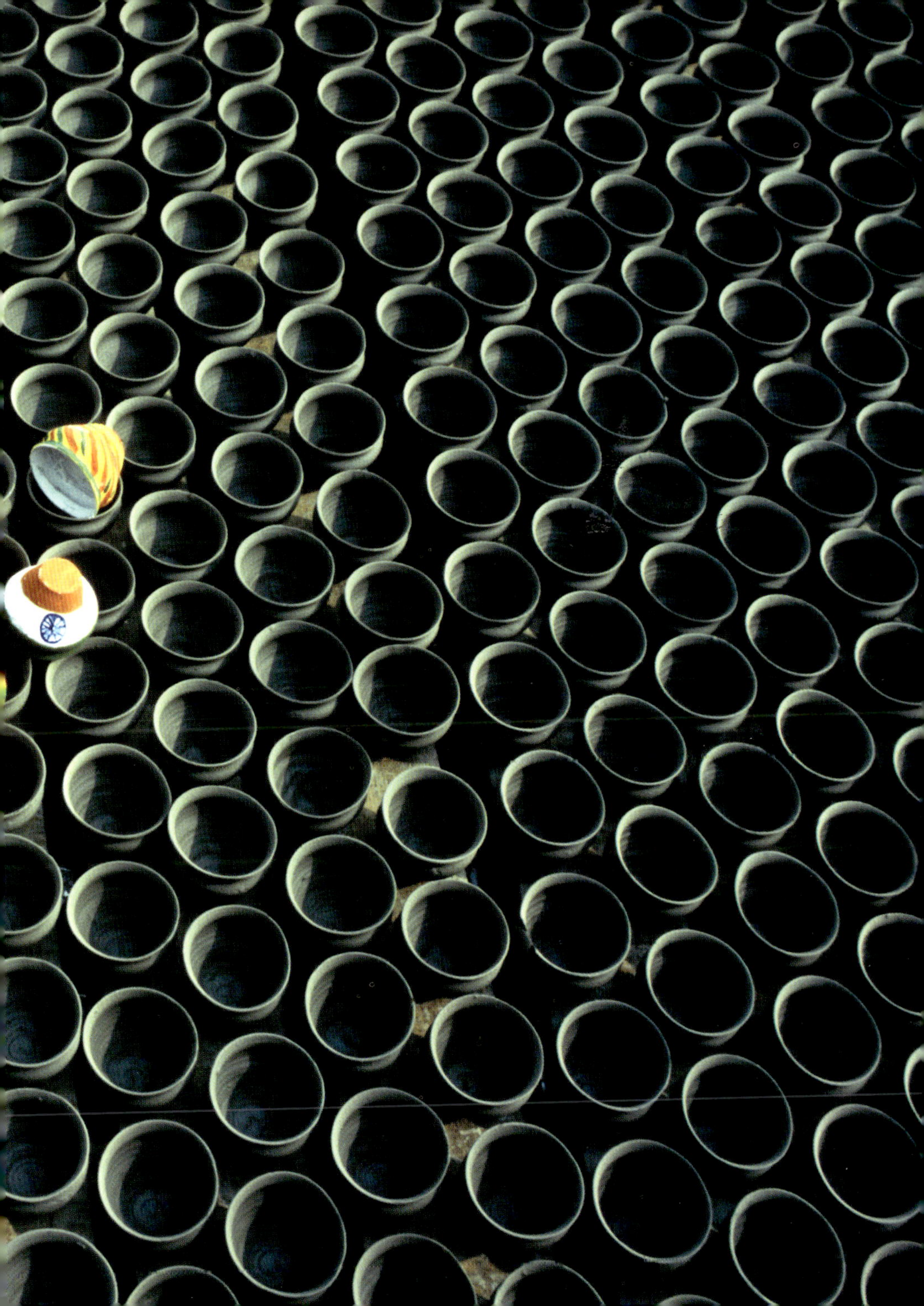

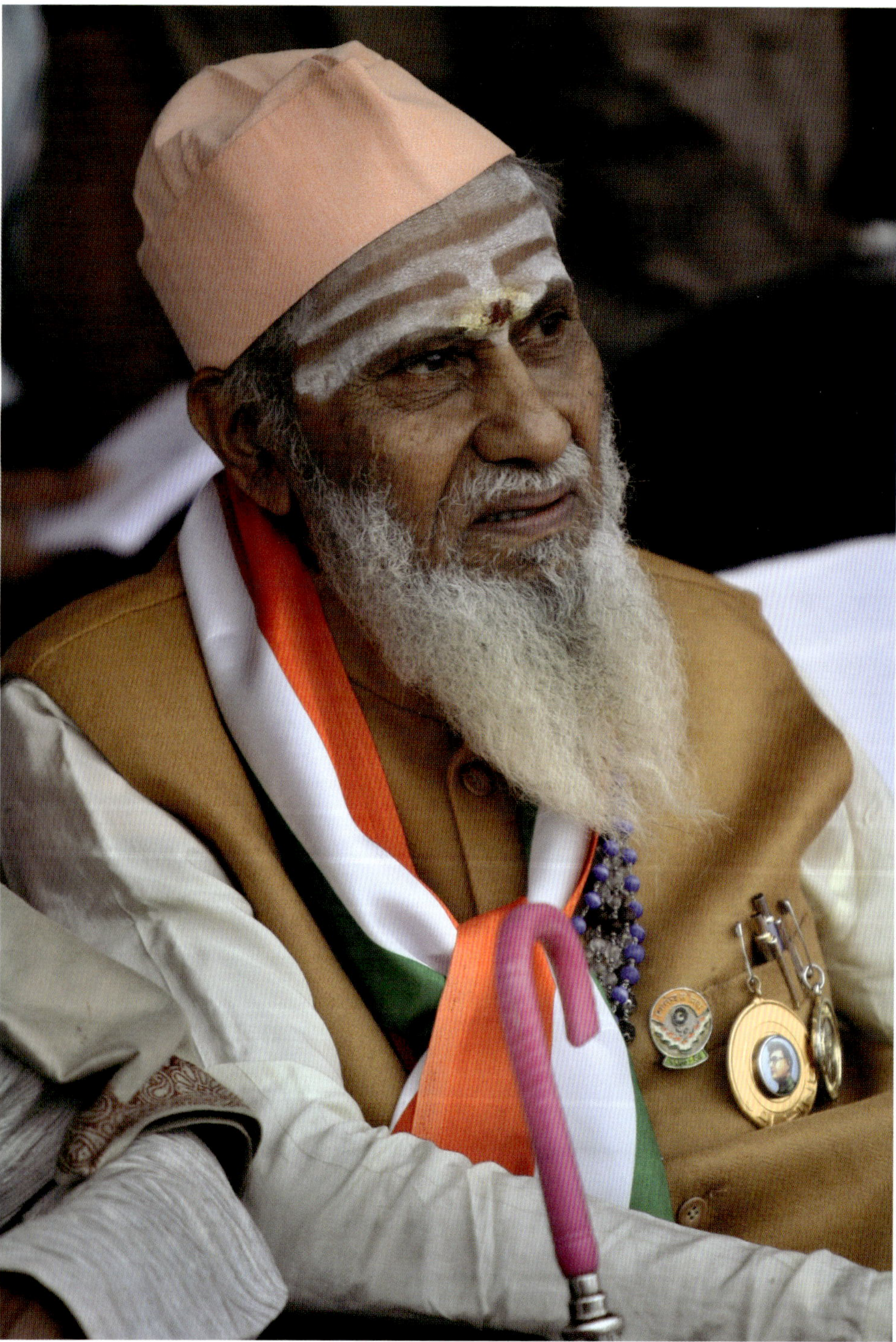

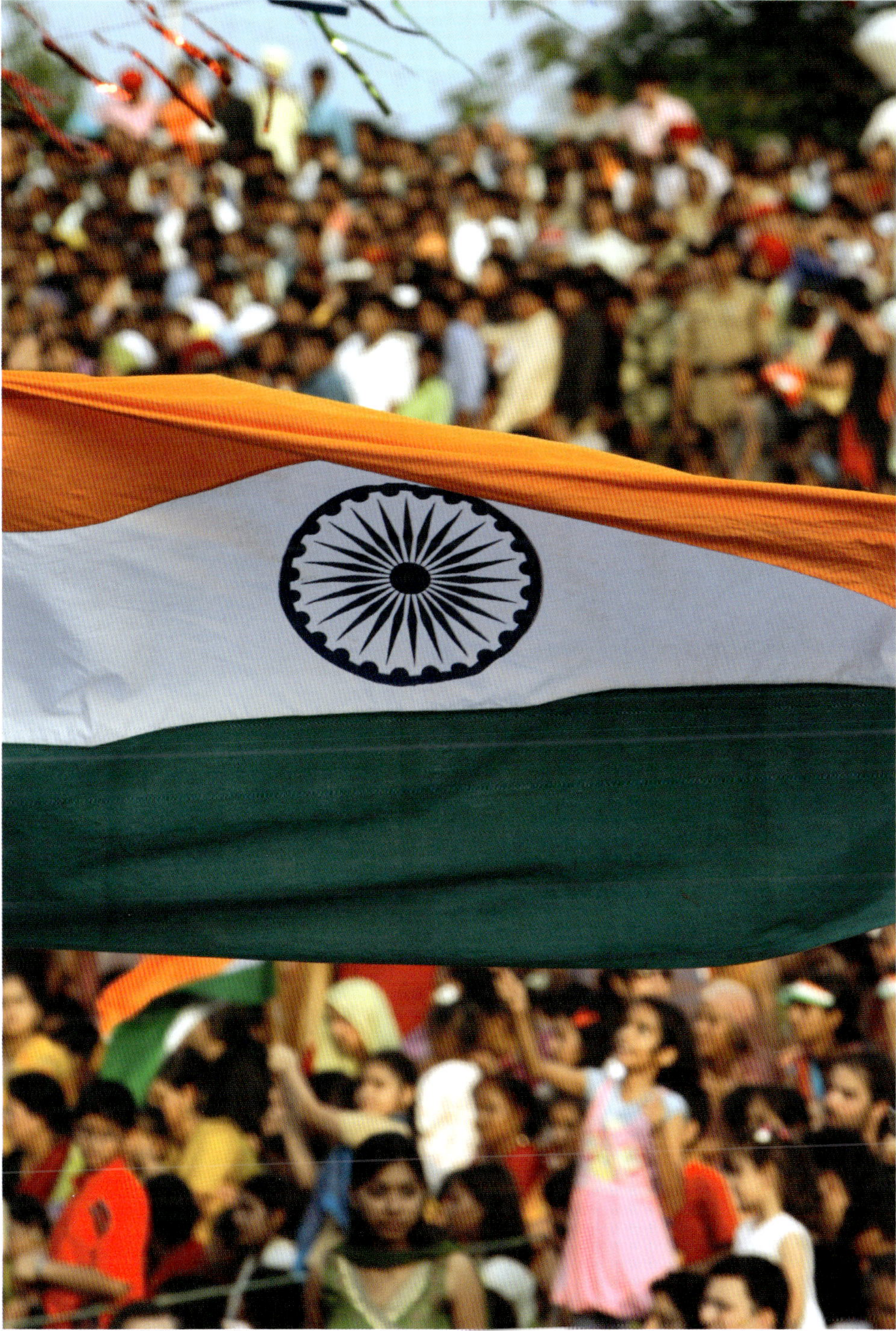

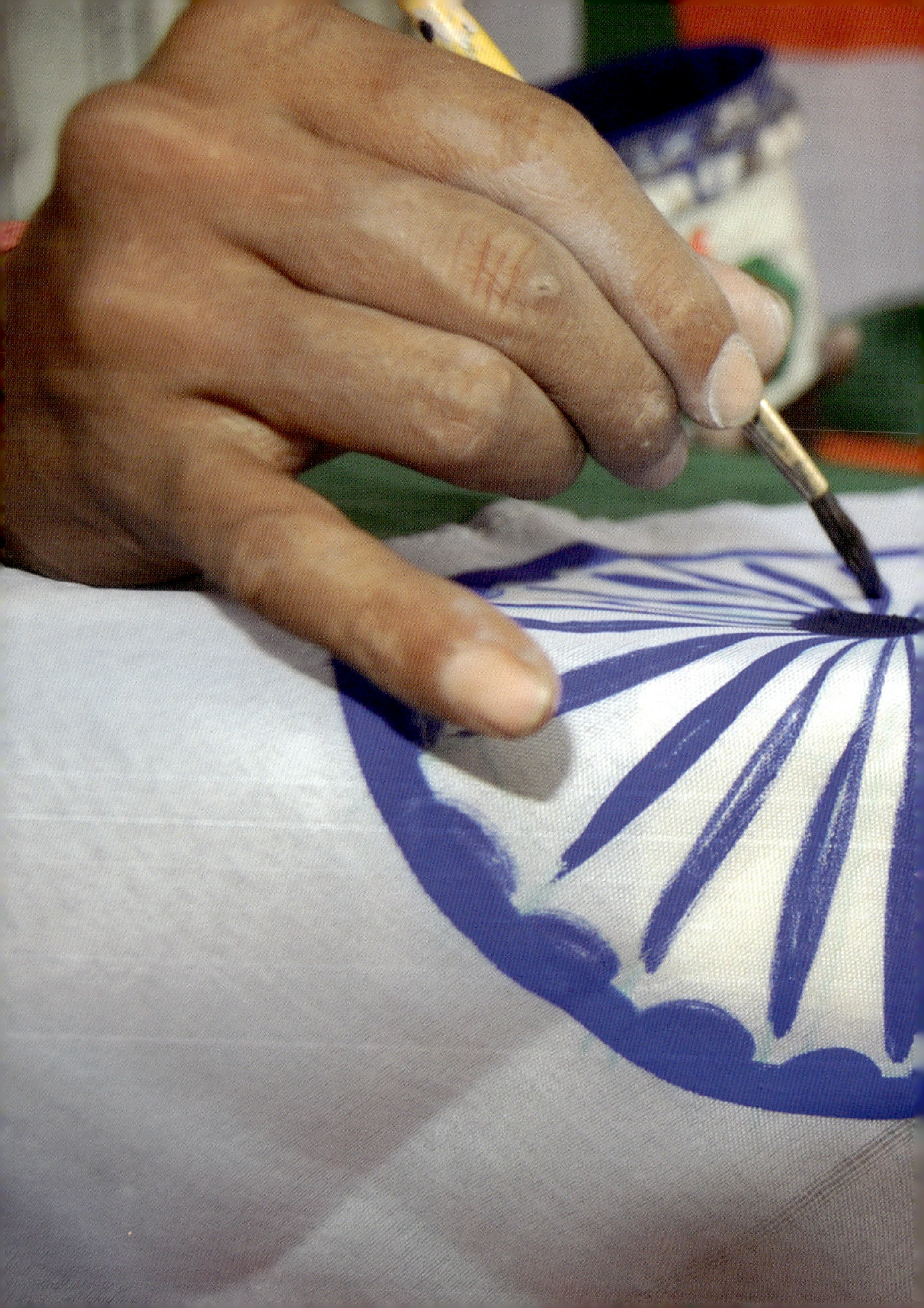

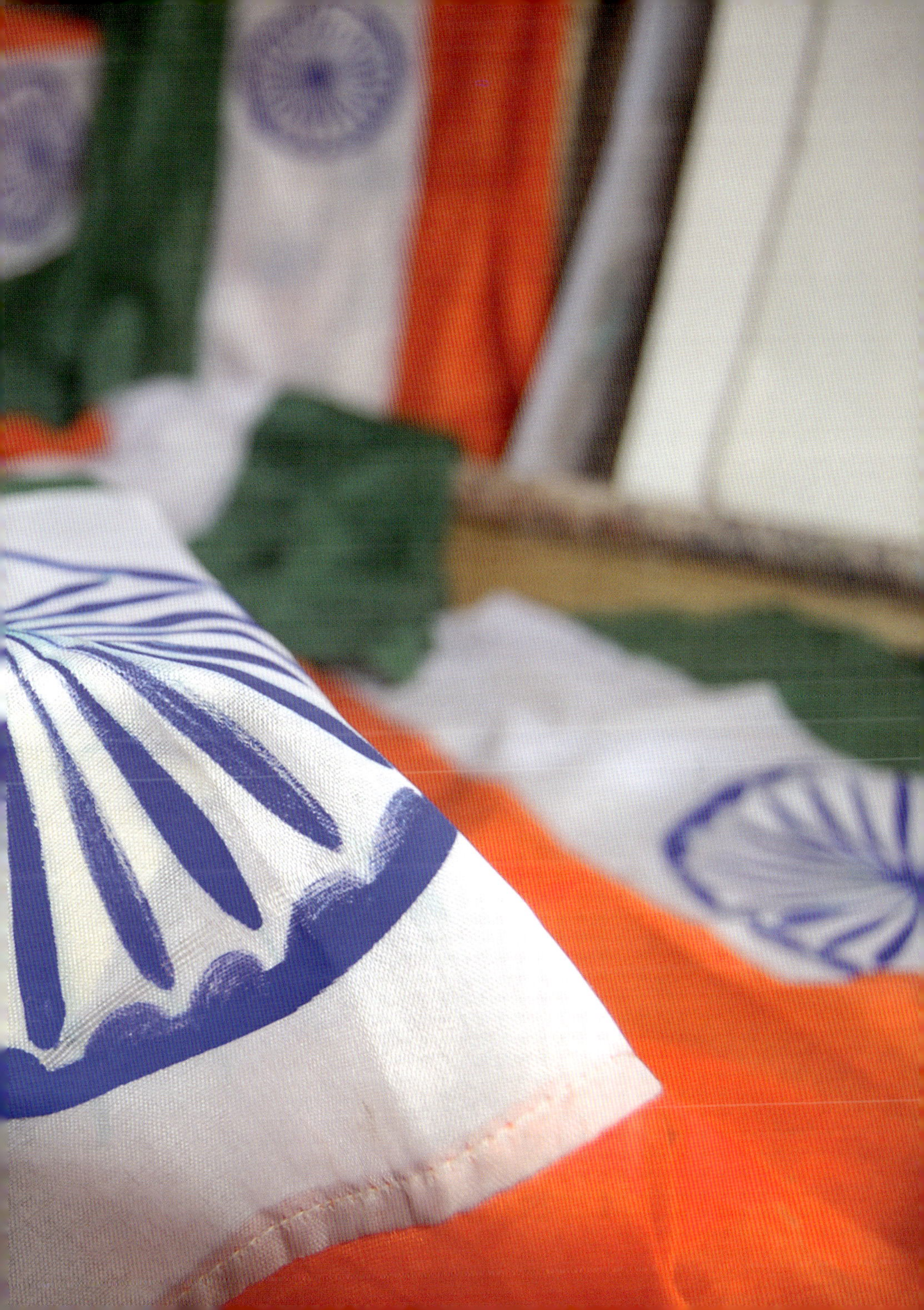

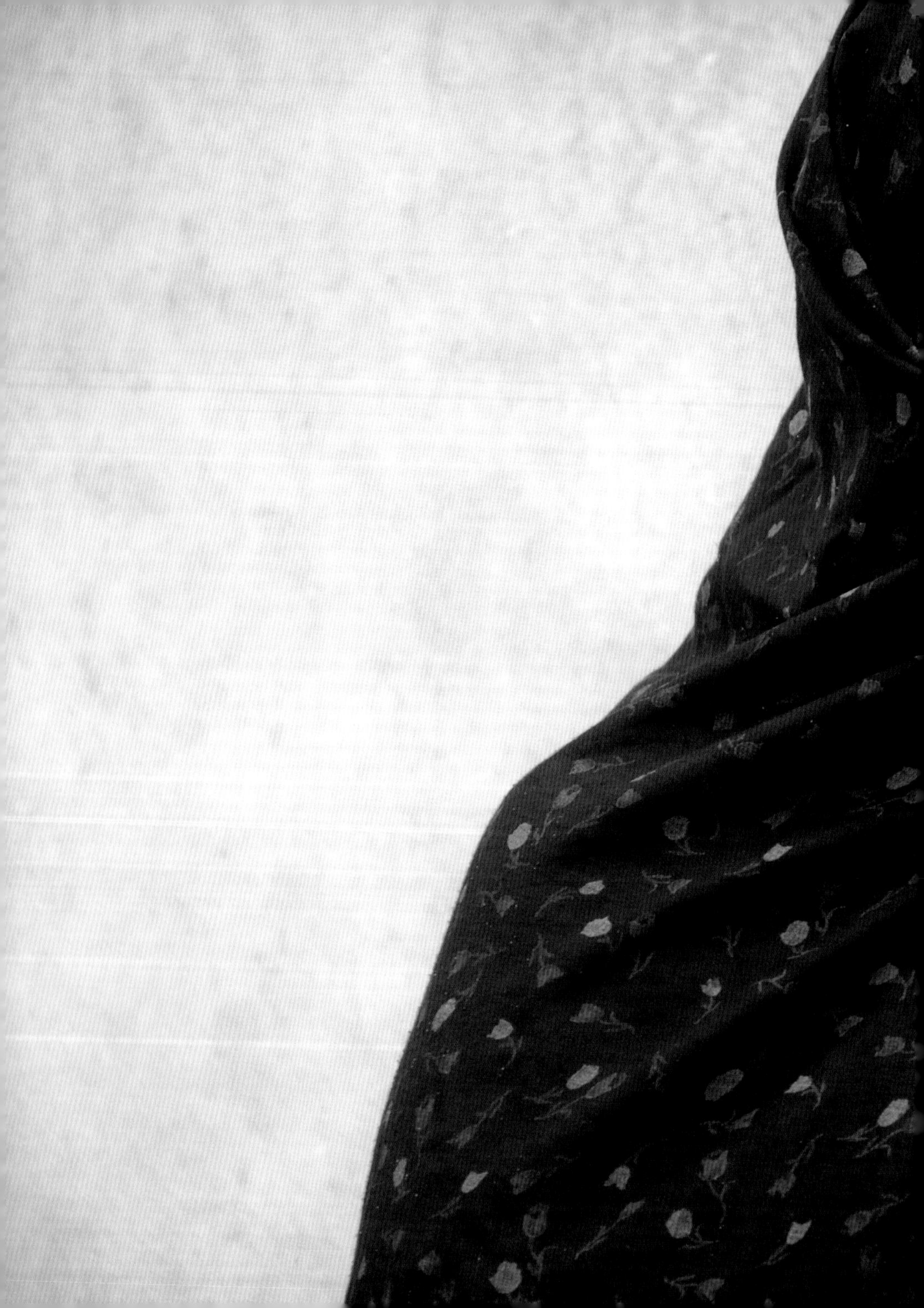

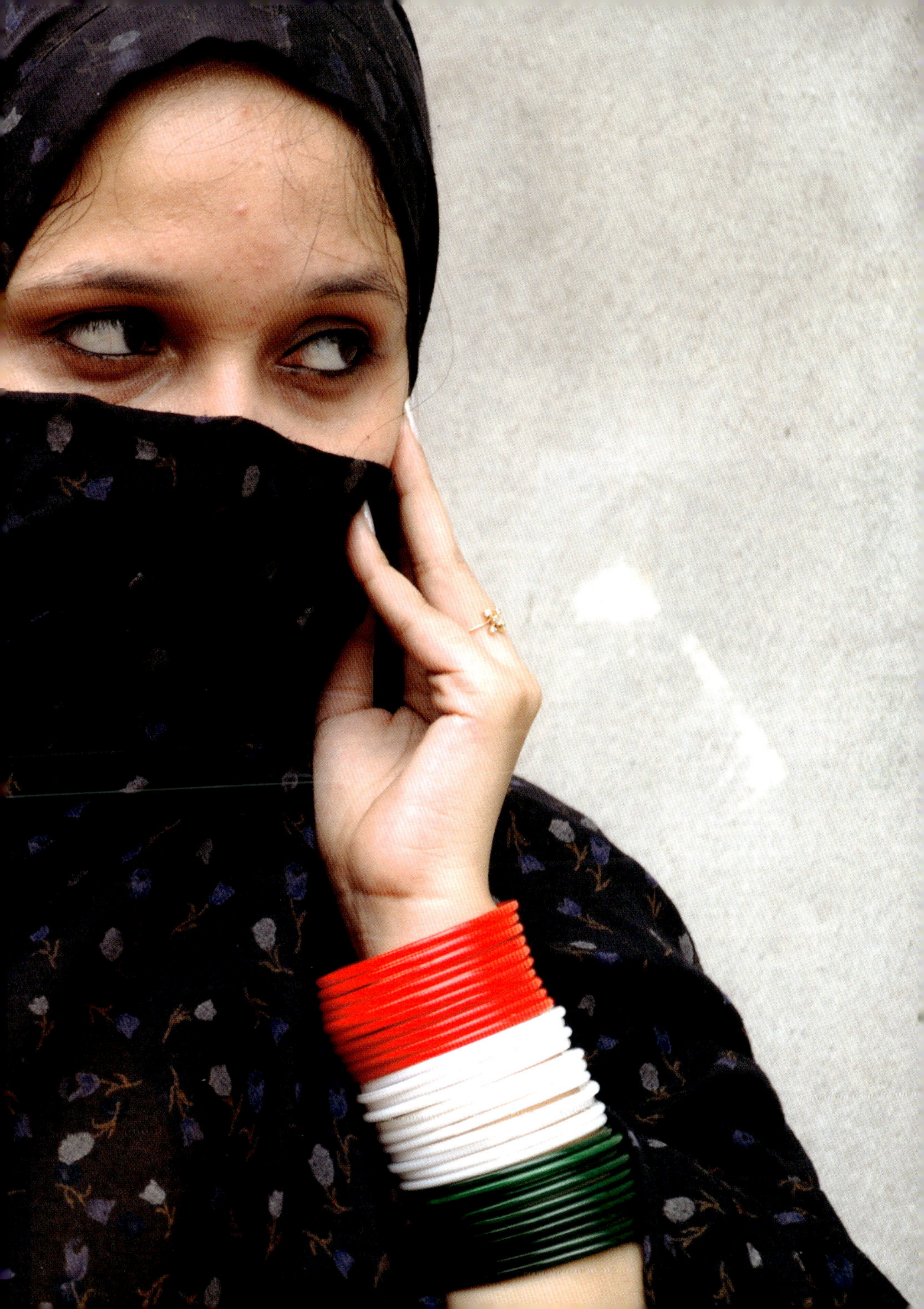

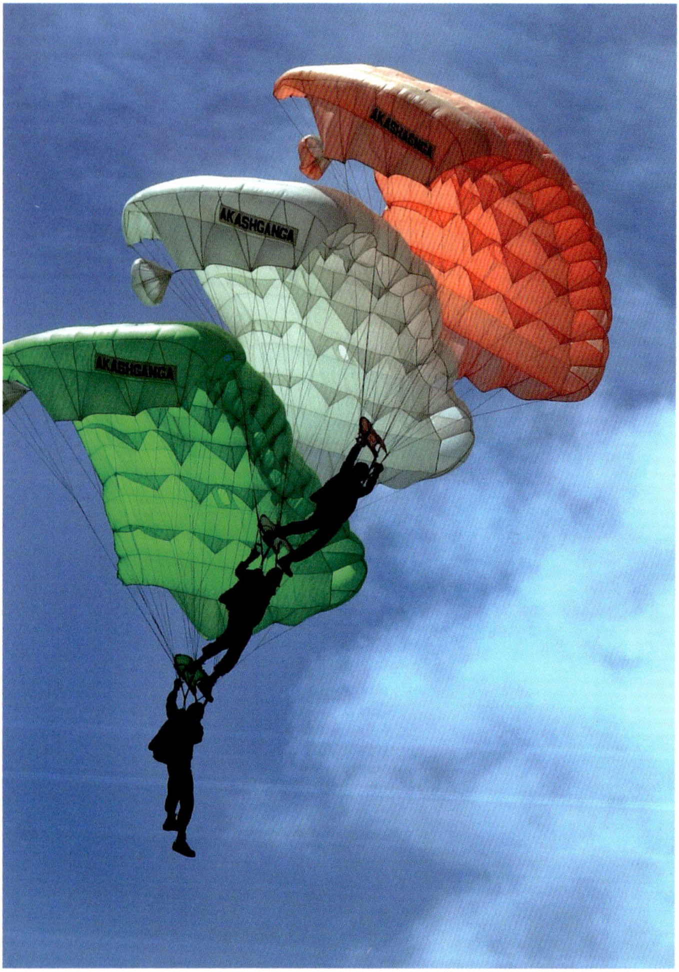

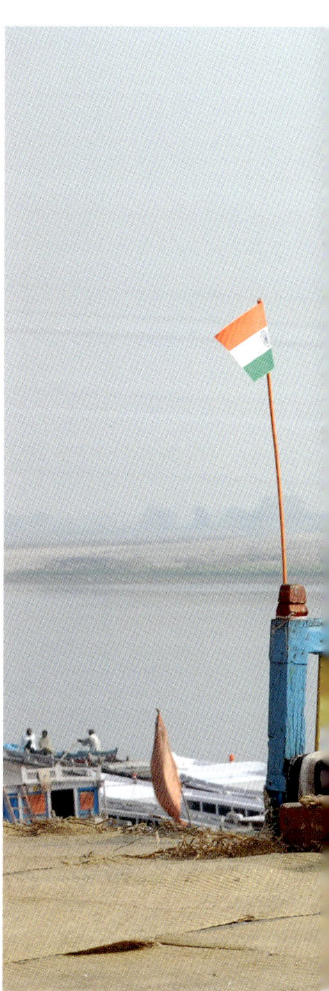

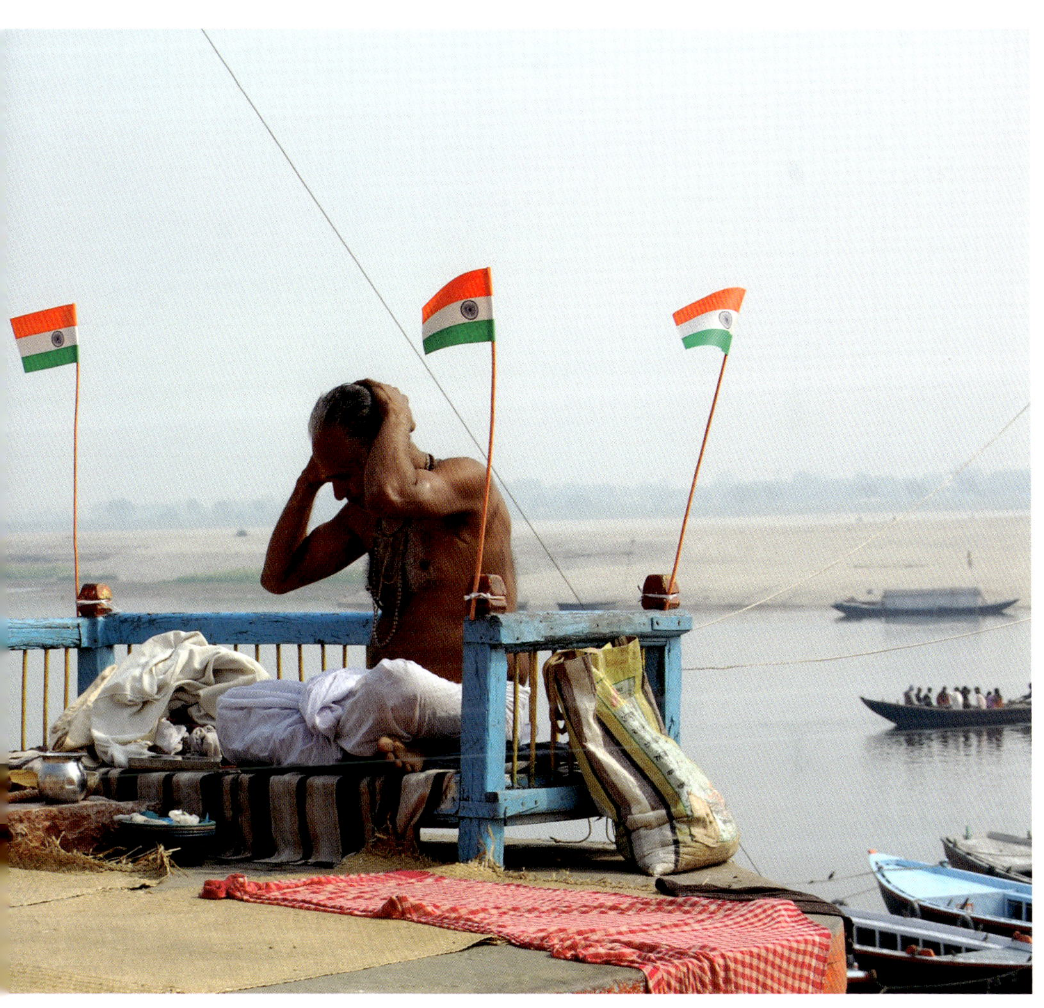

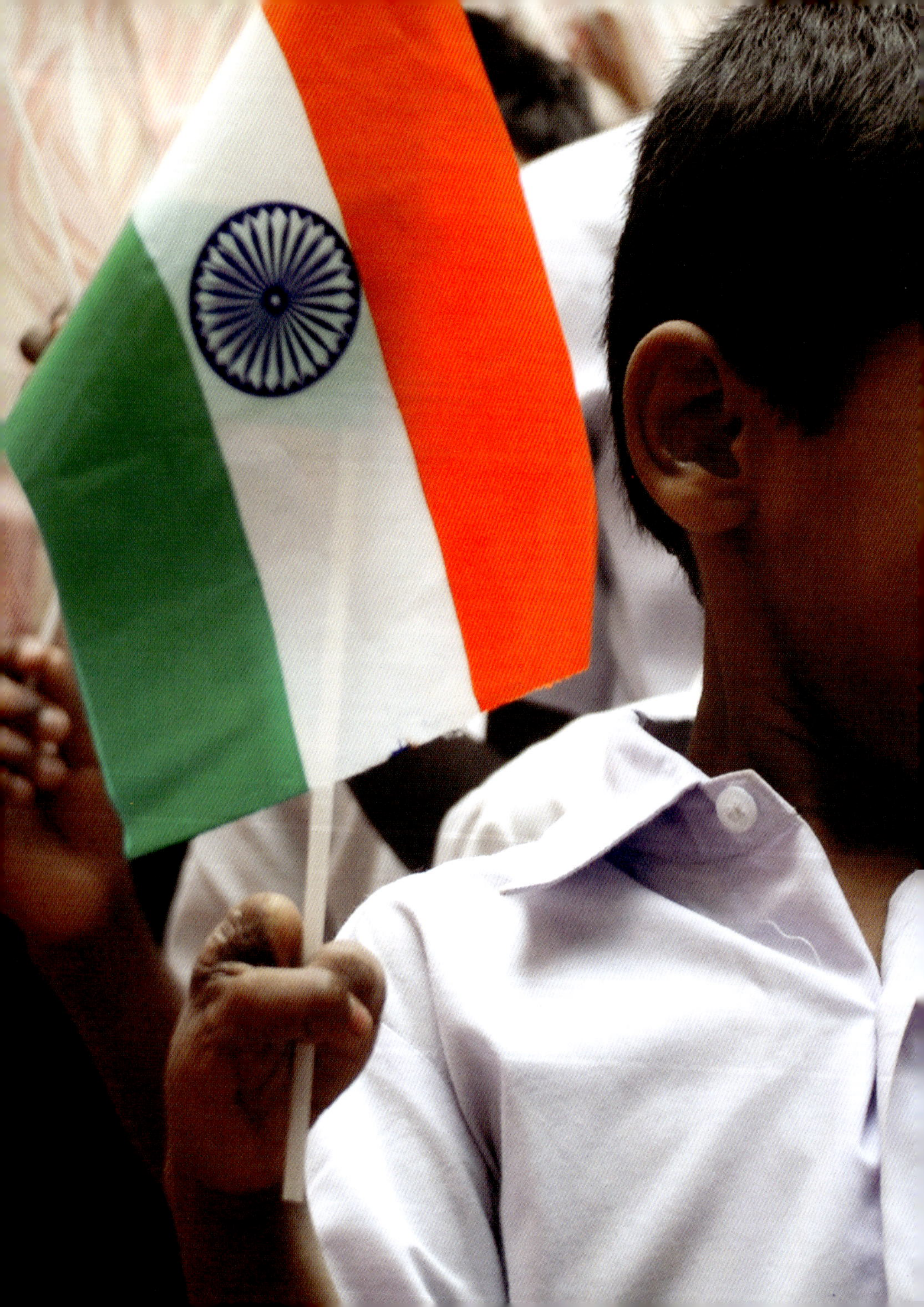

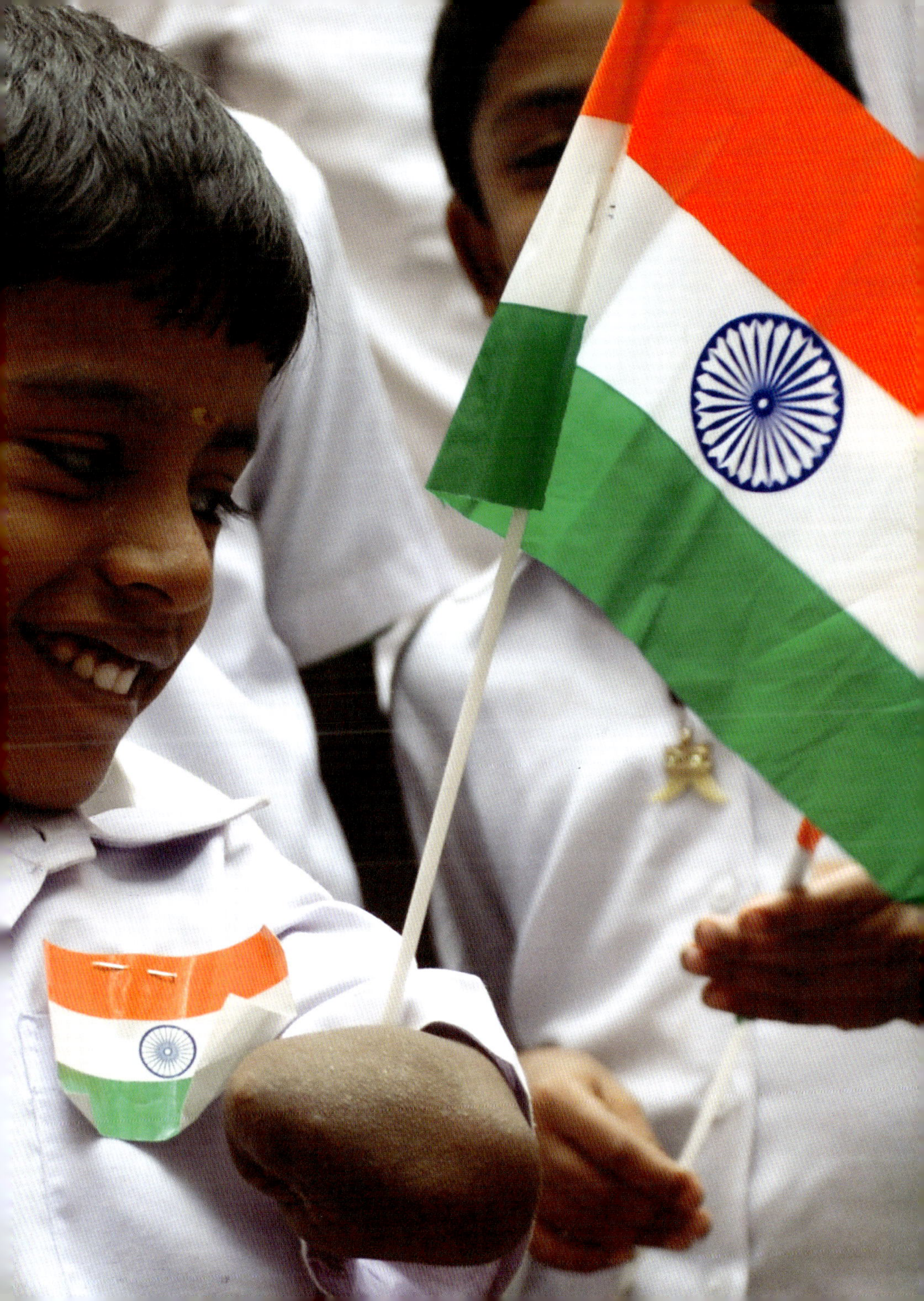

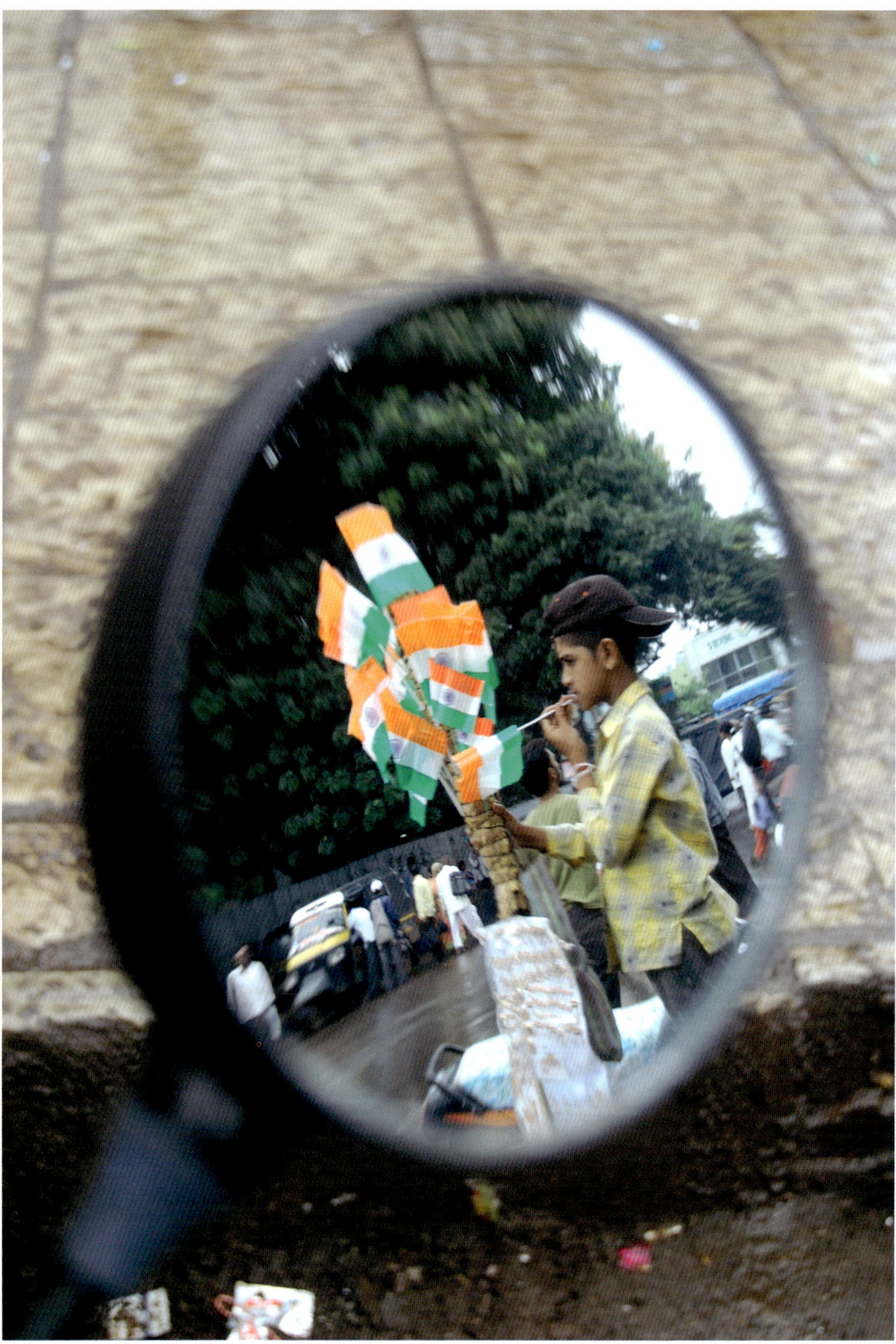

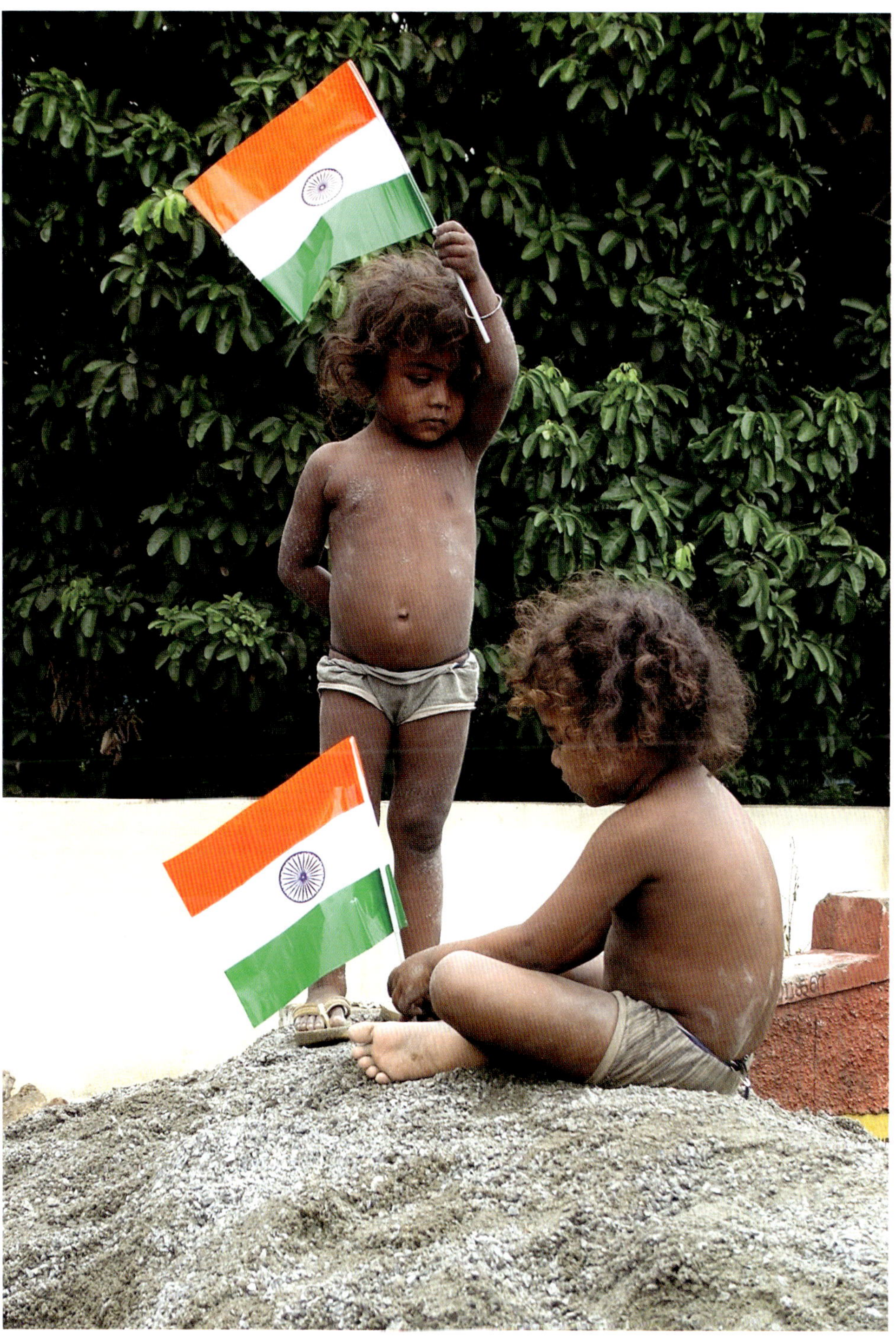

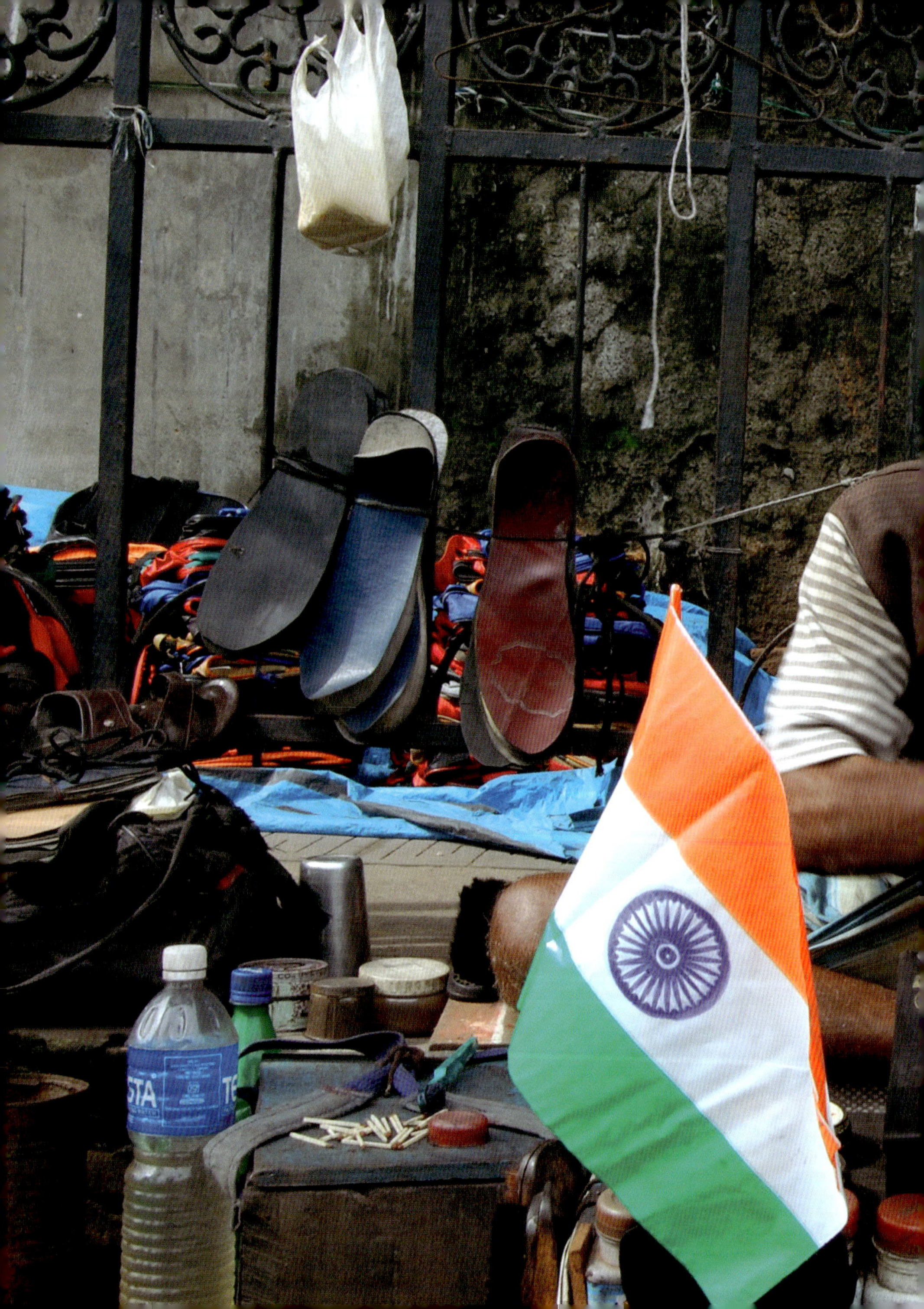

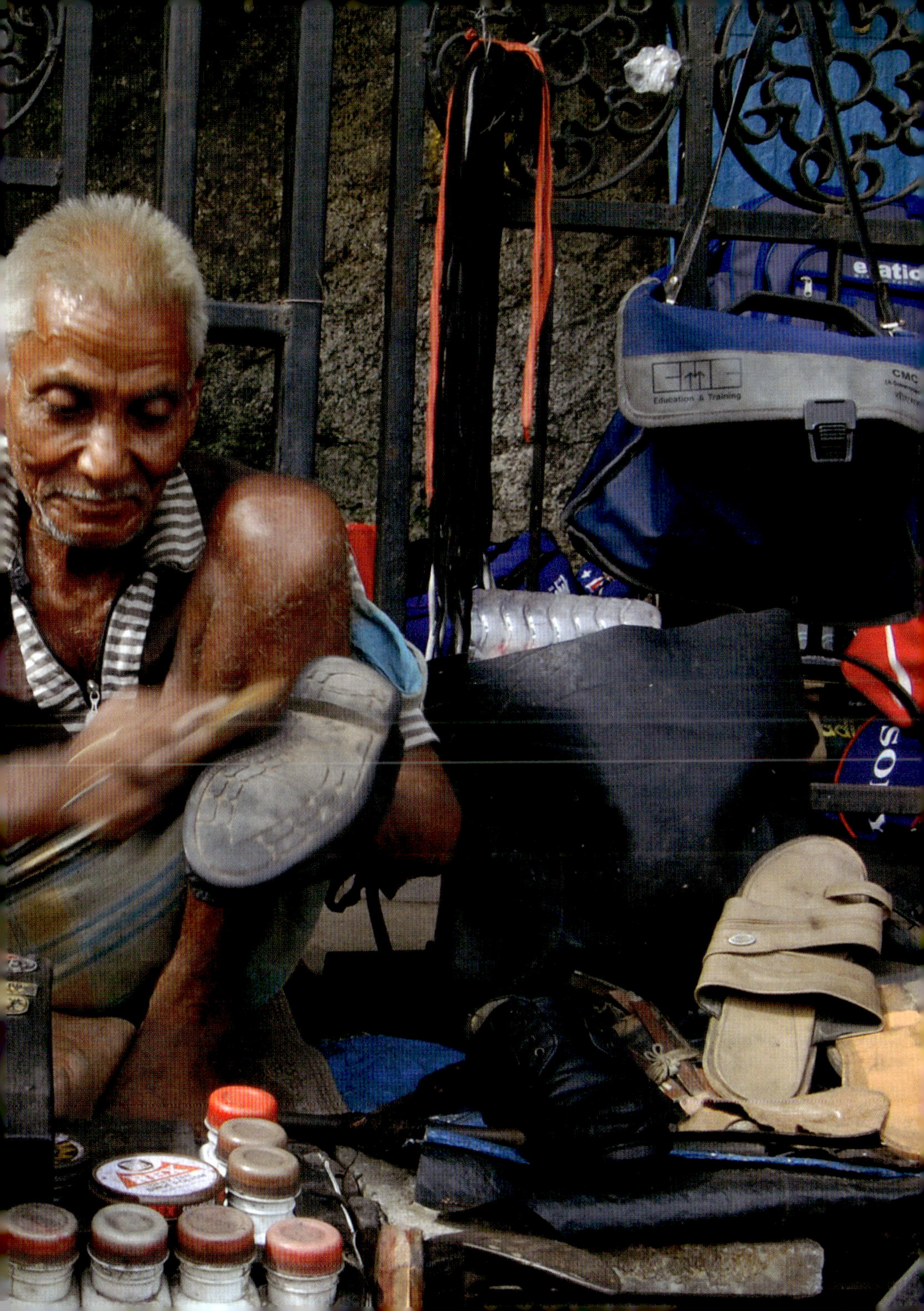

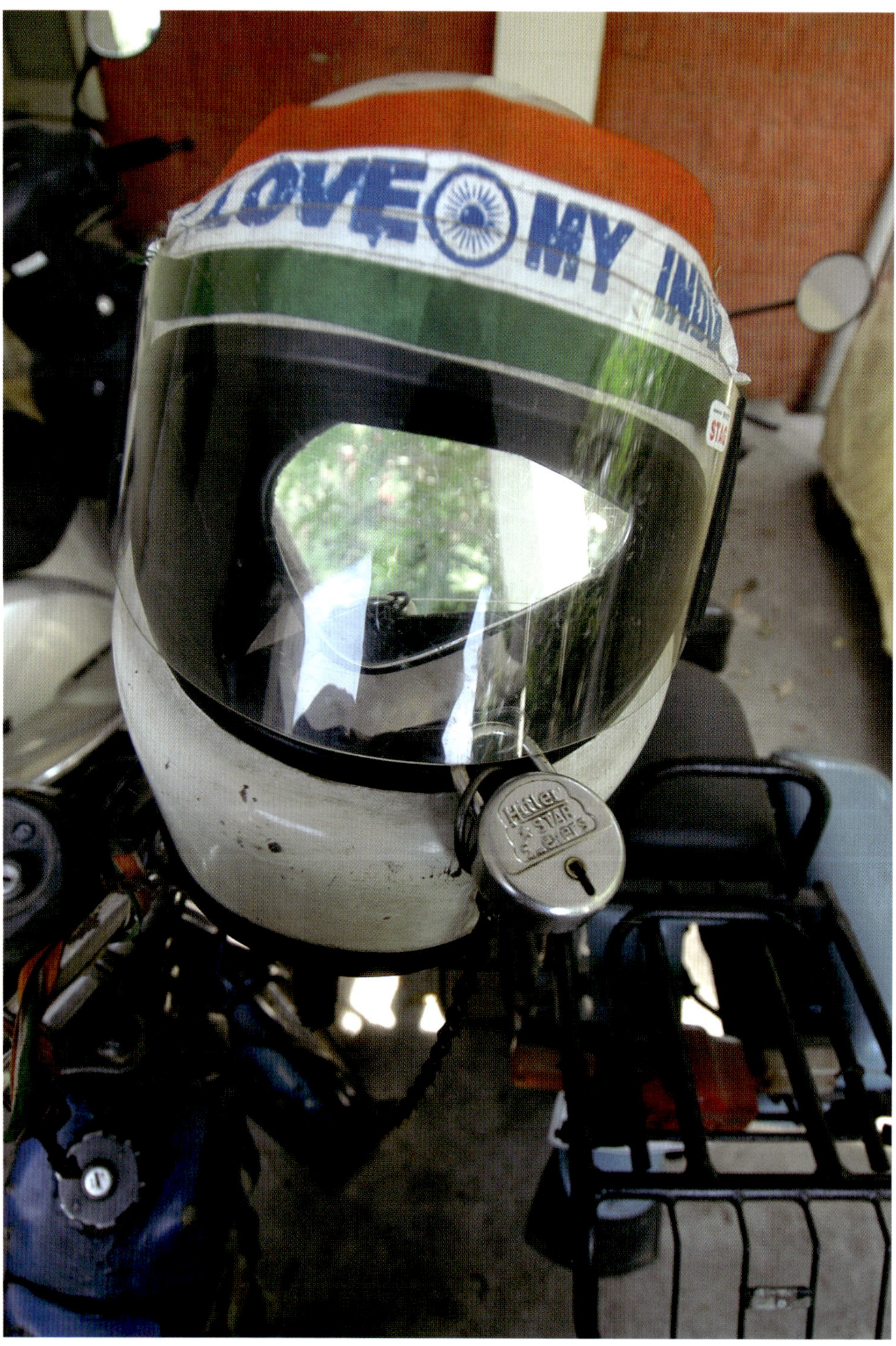
LOVE MY INDIA
STAR
Hitler
STAR

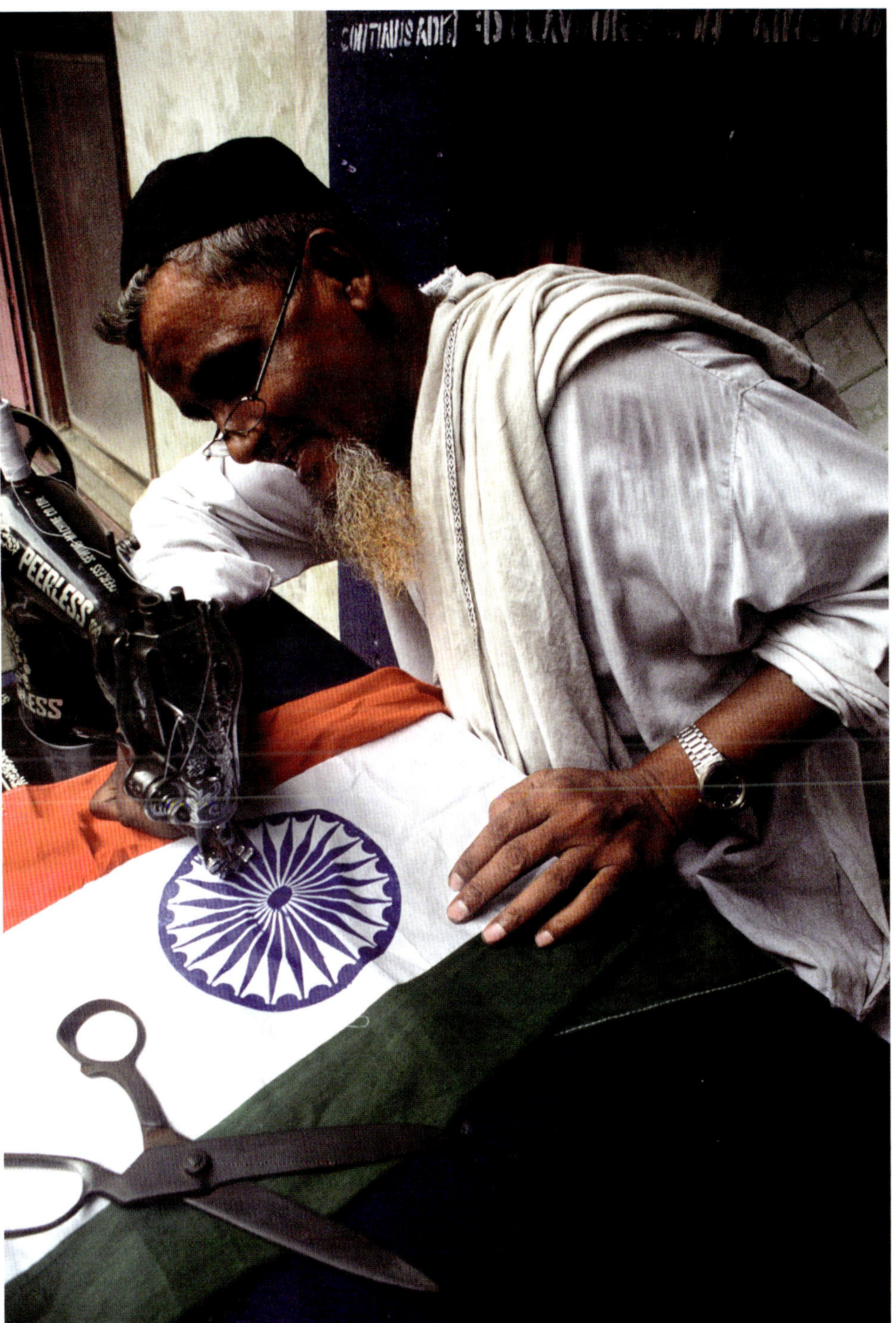

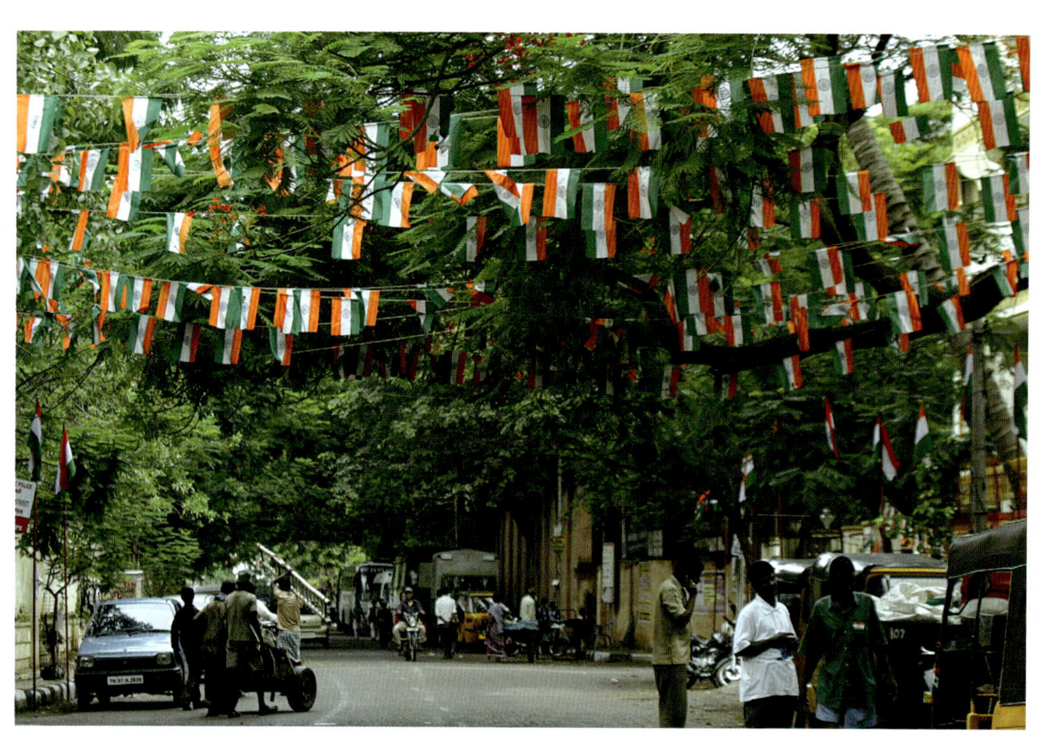

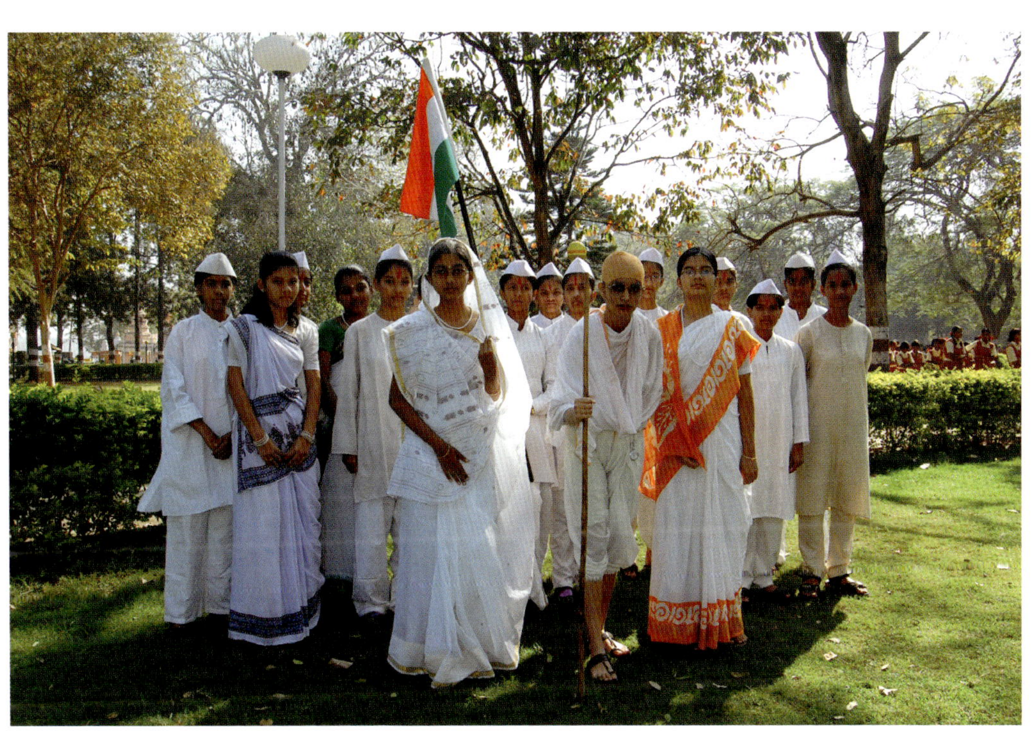

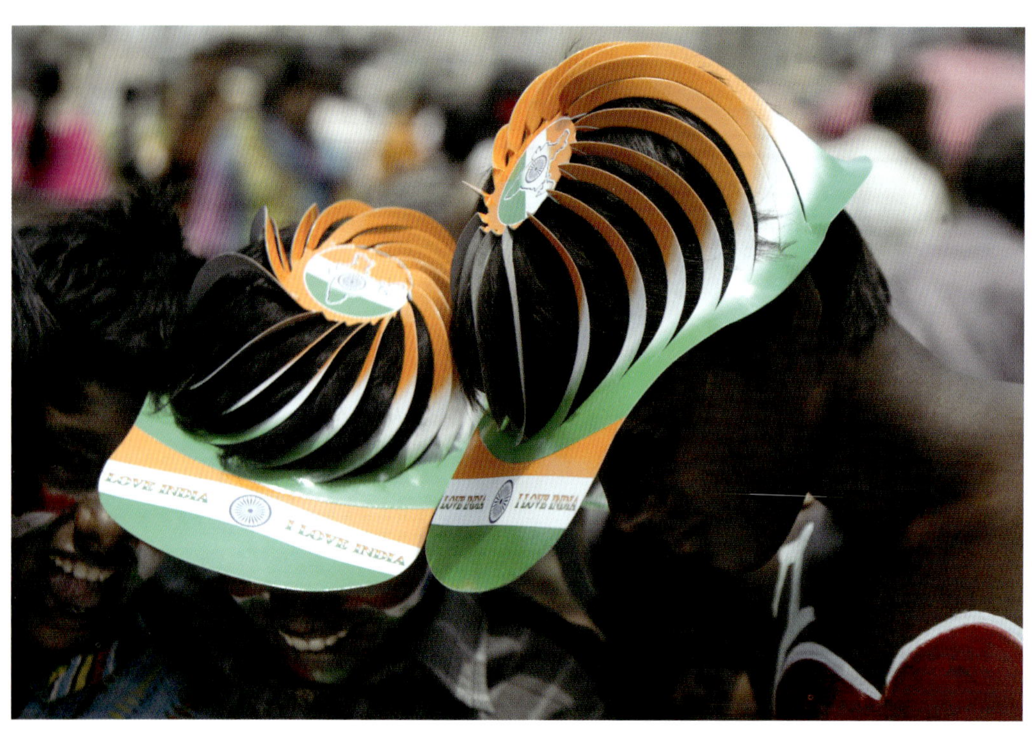

I LOVE INDIA
I LOVE INDIA
I LOVE INDIA
I LOVE INDIA

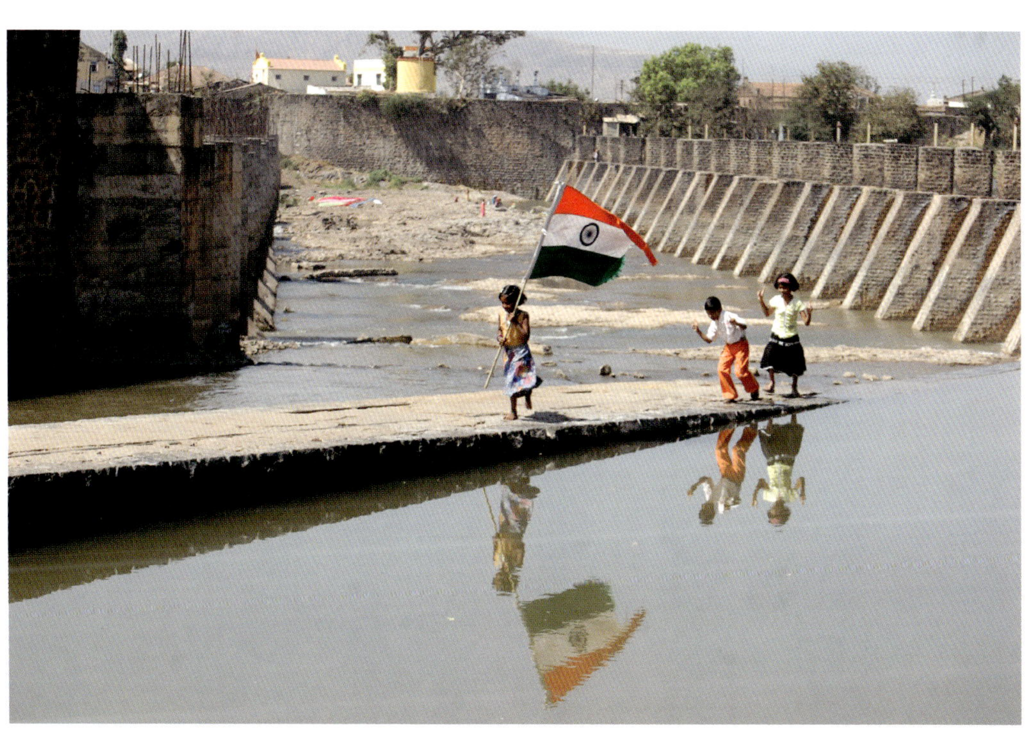

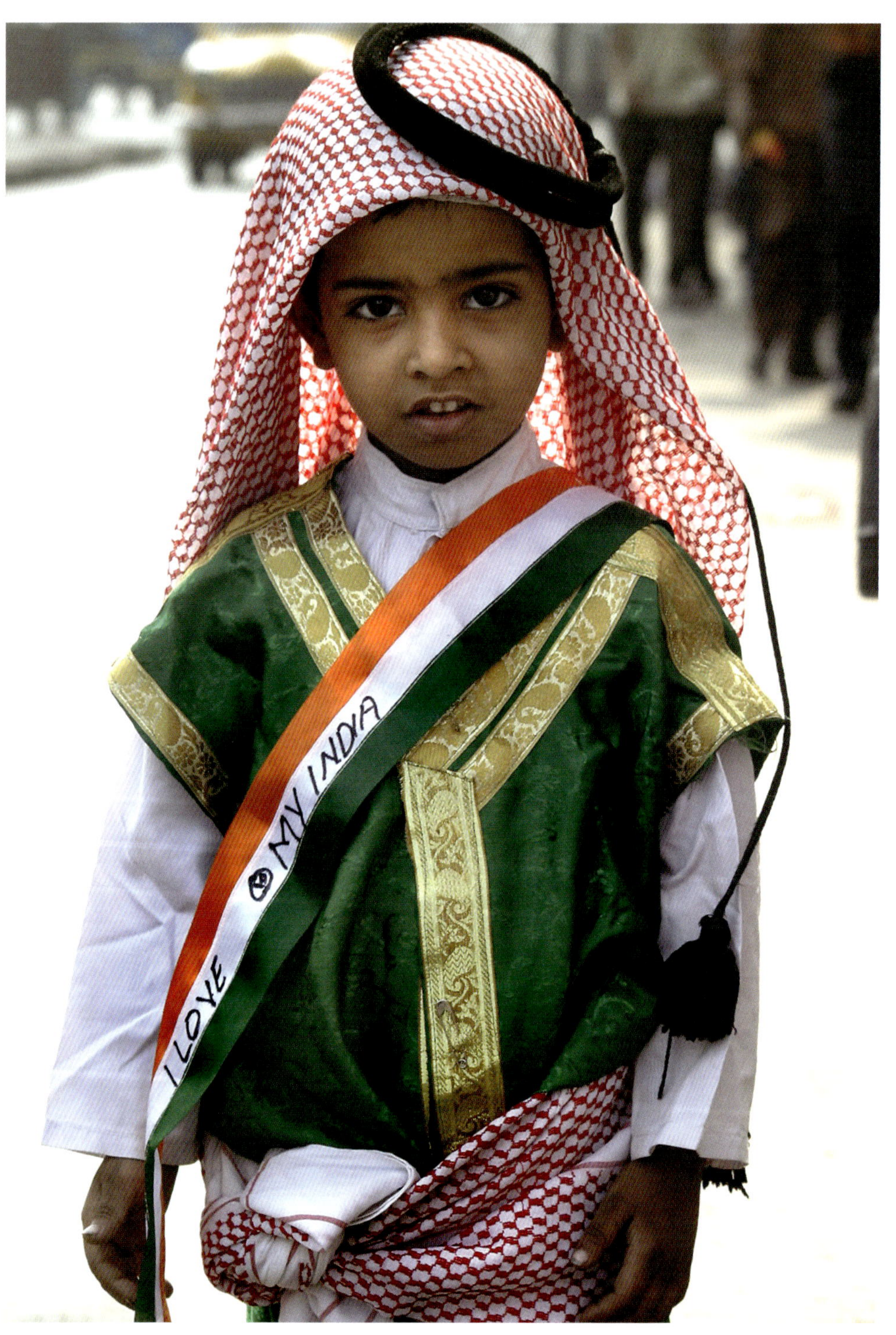

I LOVE MY INDIA

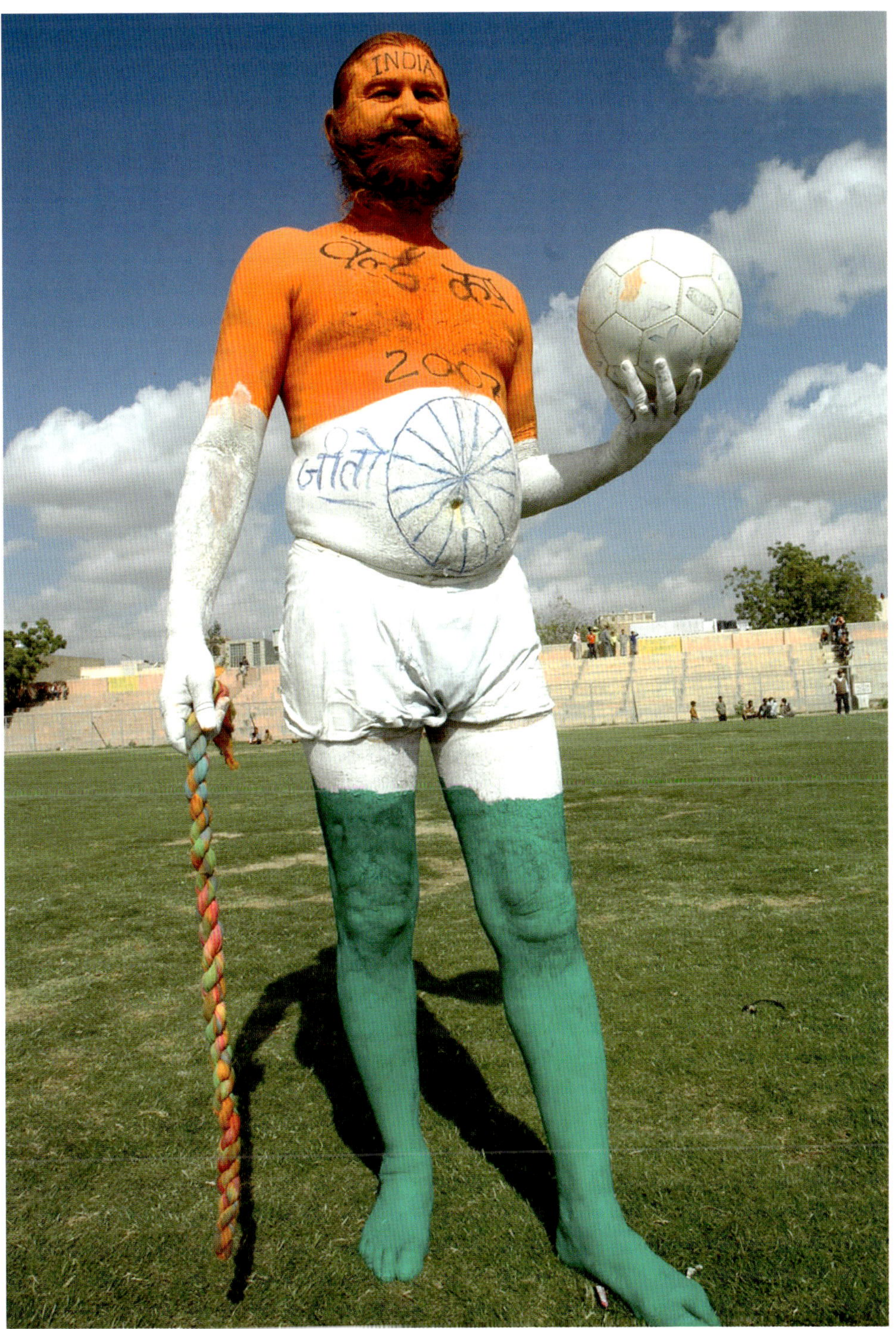
INDIA
वेल्ड कप
2007
जीतो

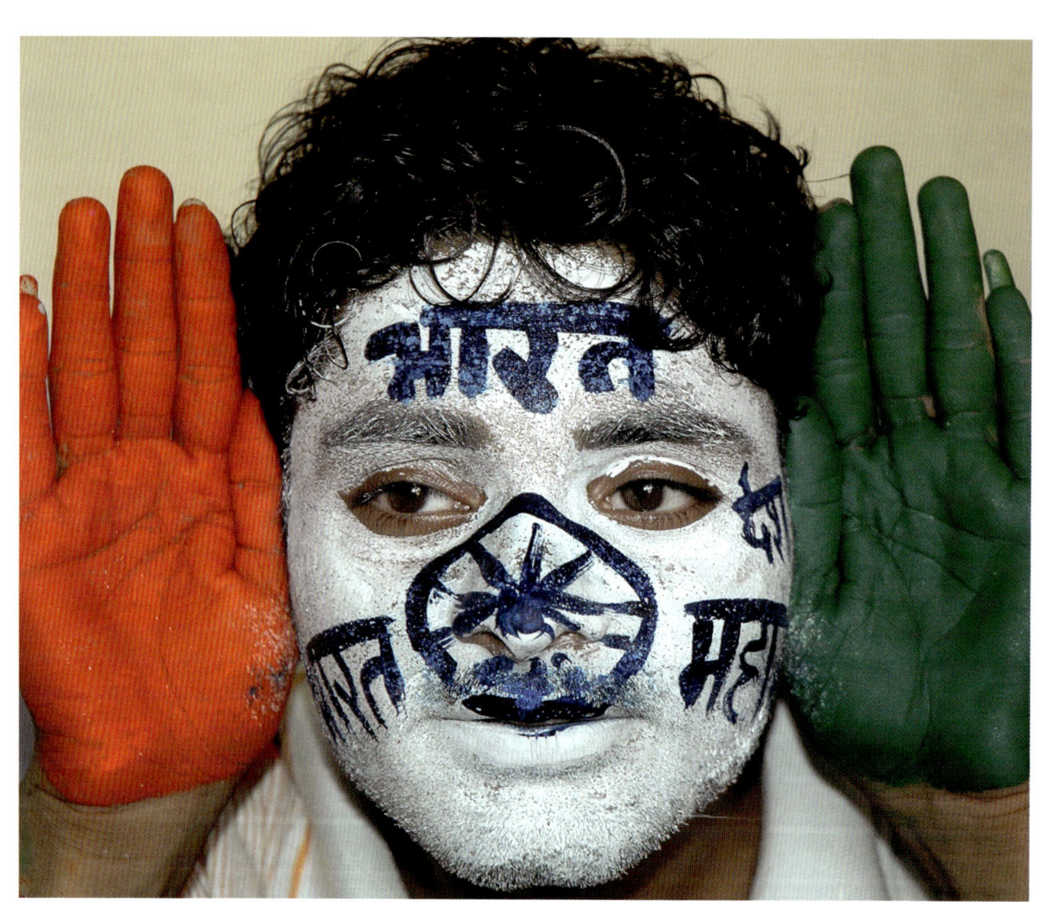

भारत
भारत
भारत

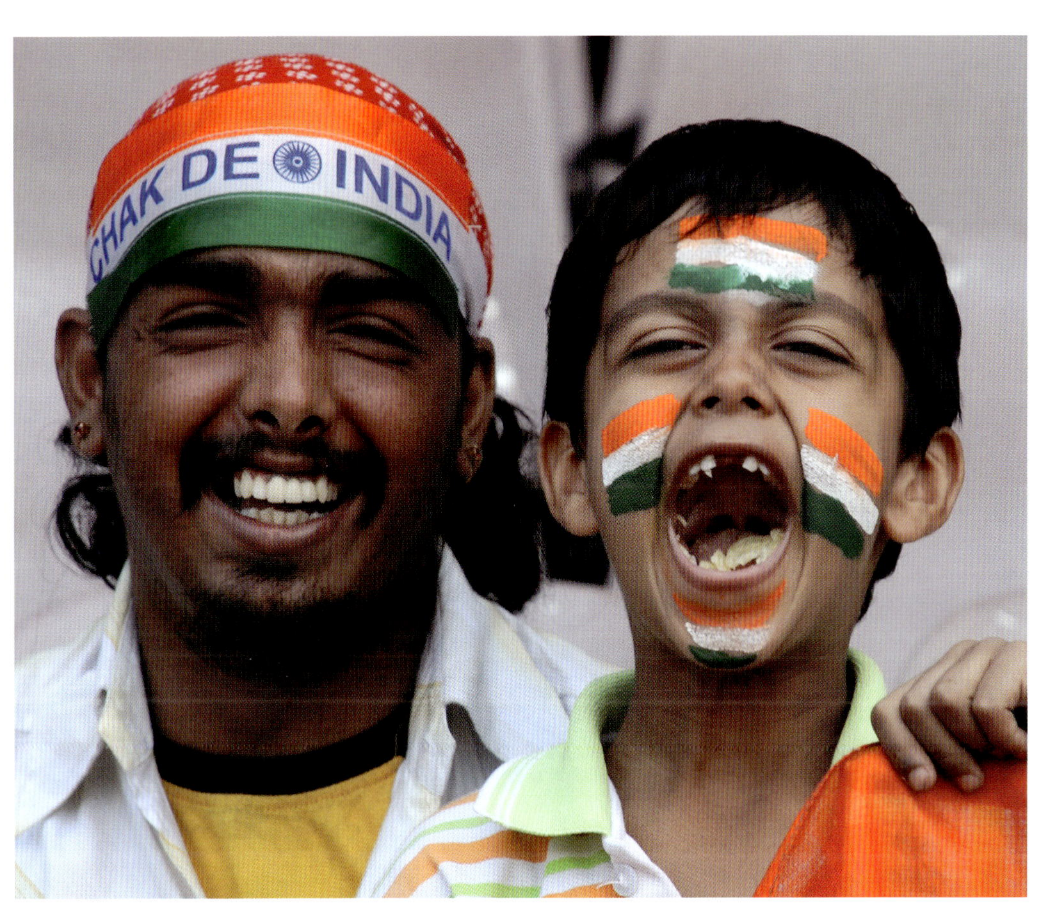

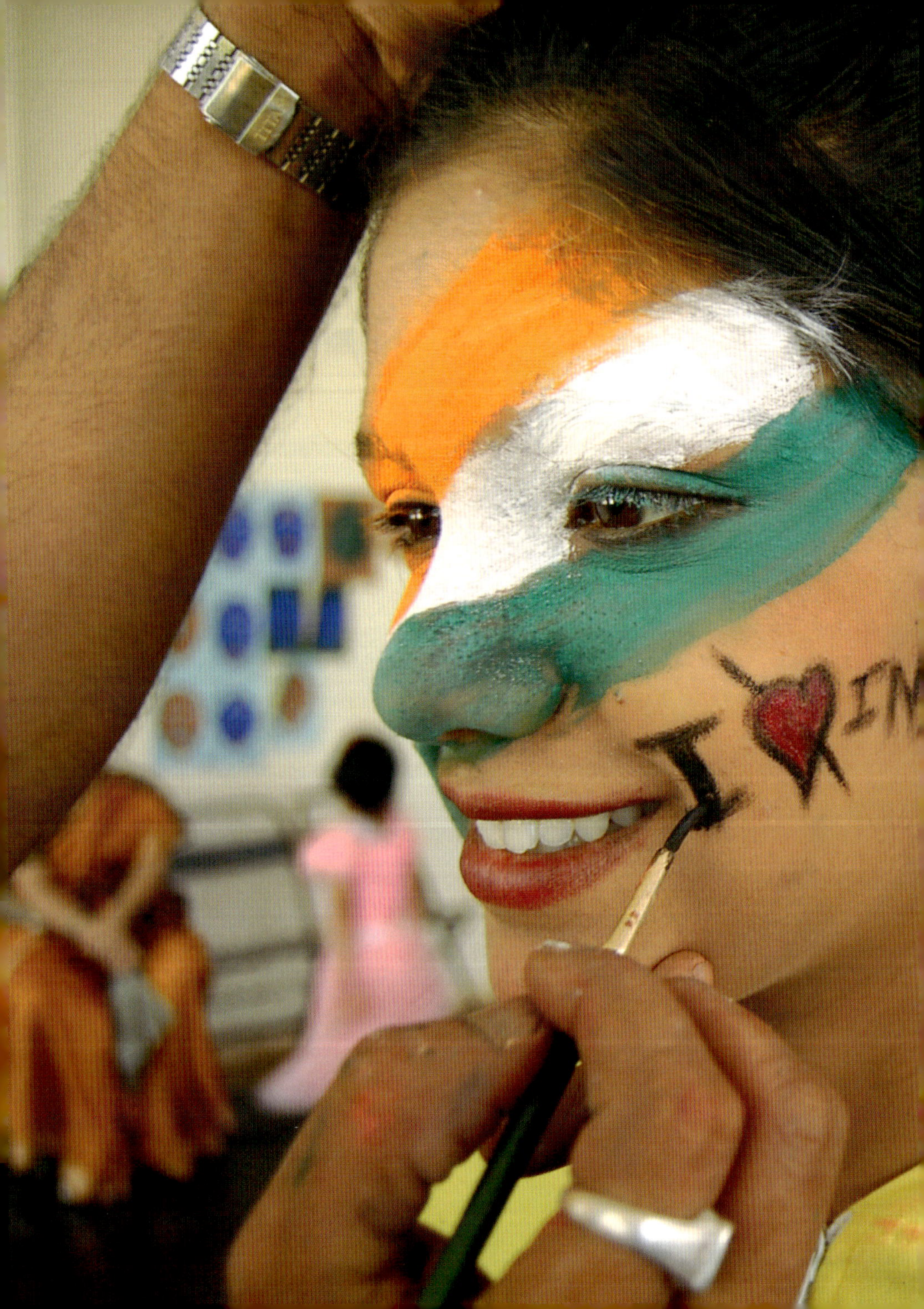

I ♥ IN

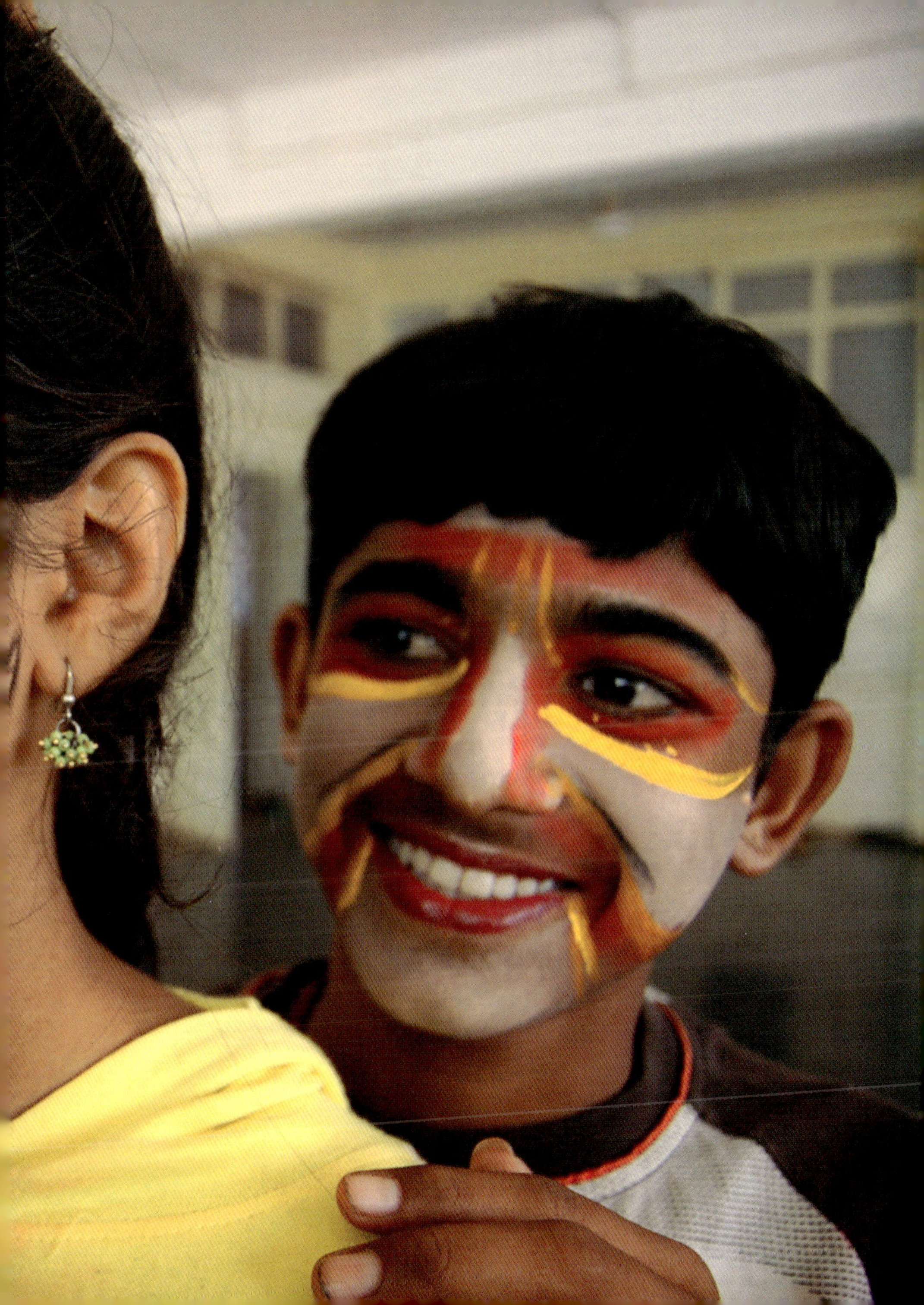

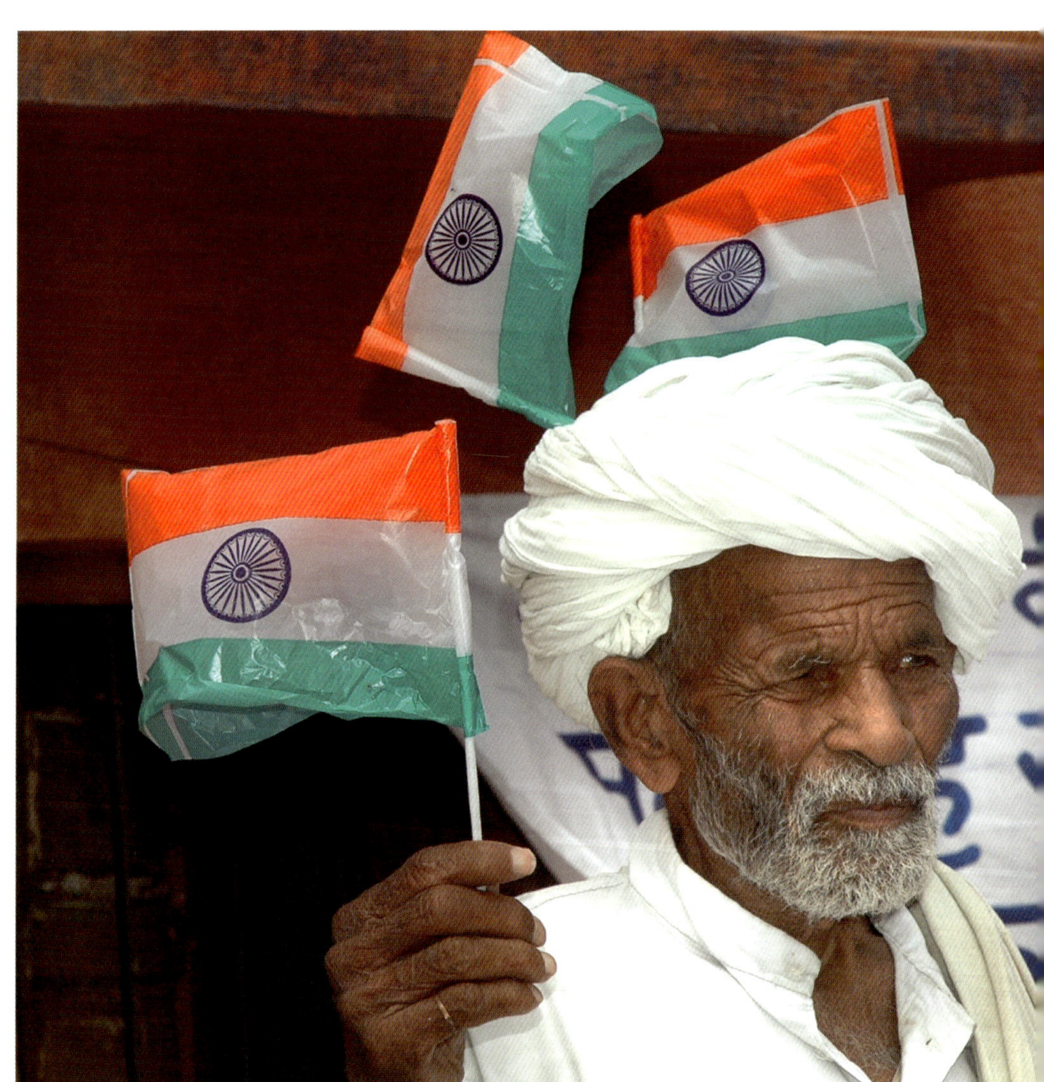

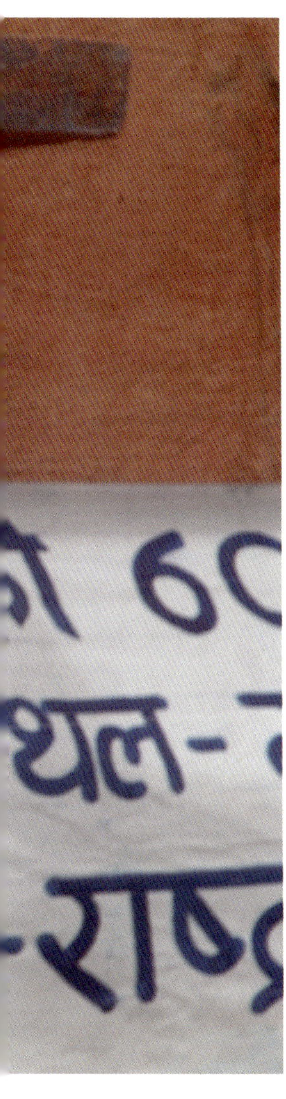
60
थल-
-राष्ट्र

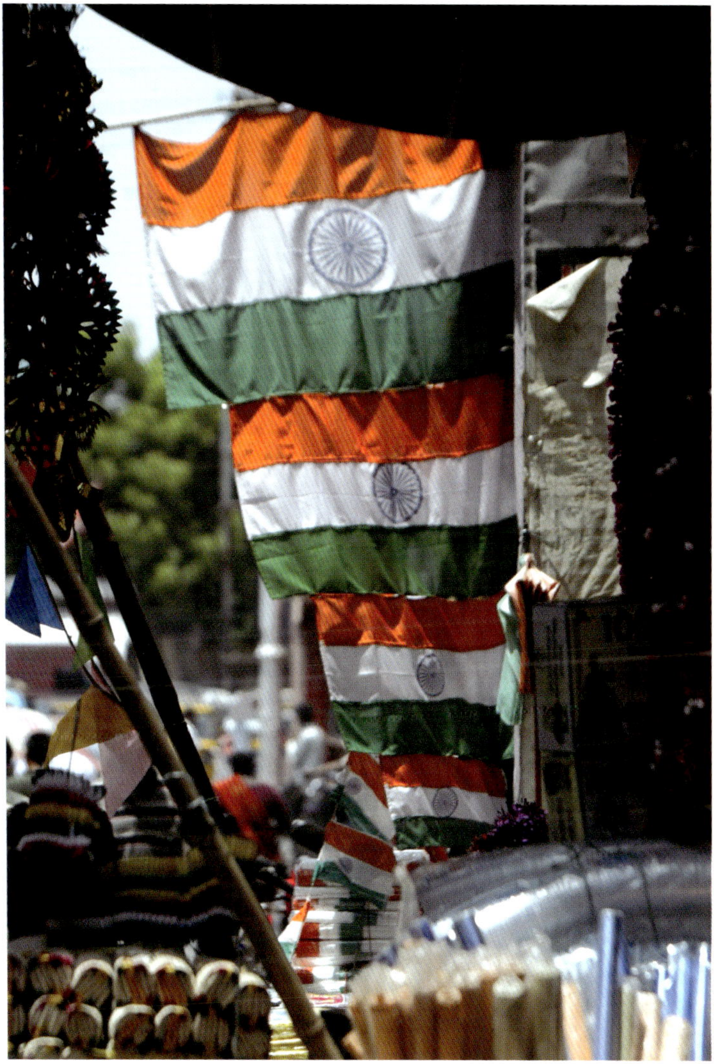

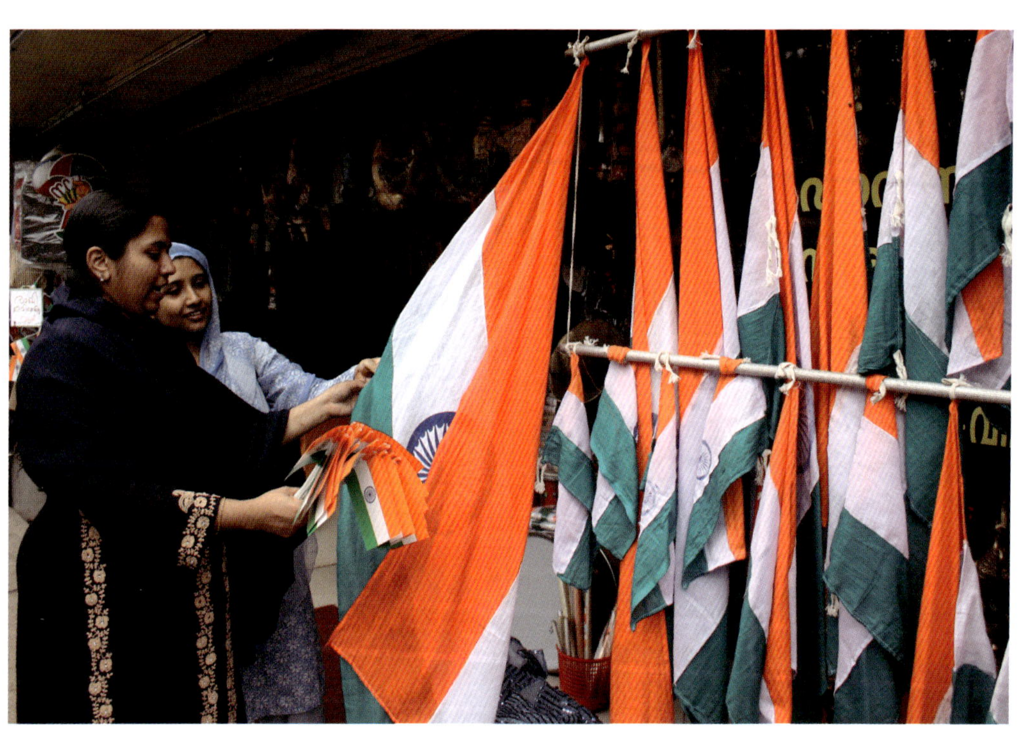

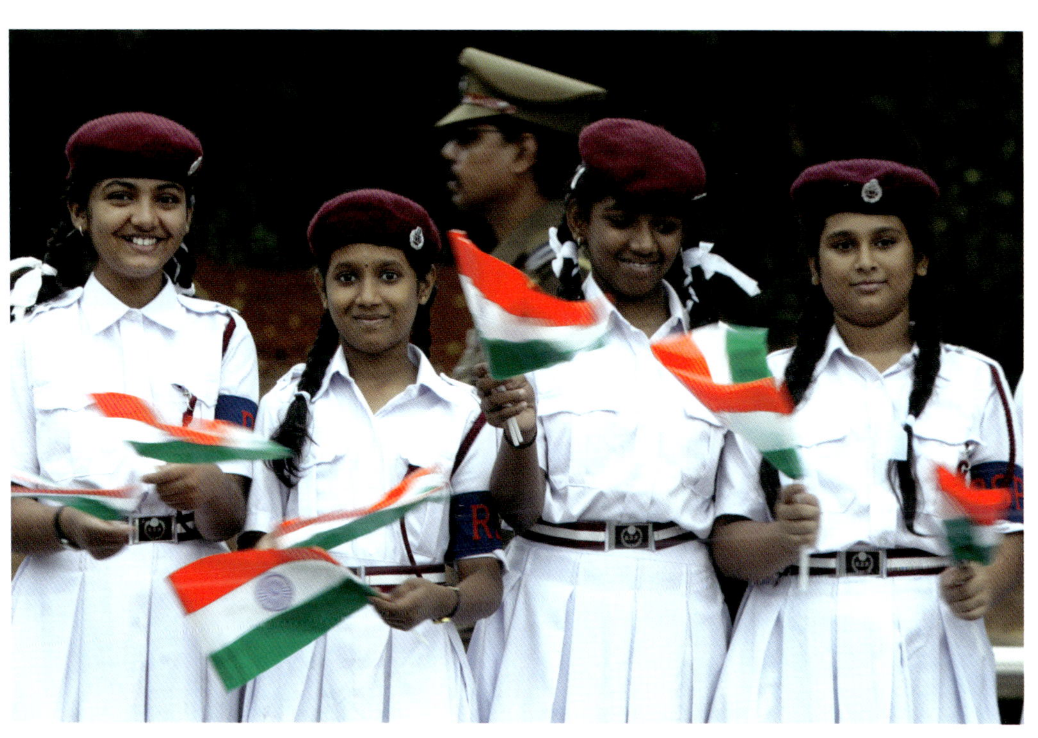

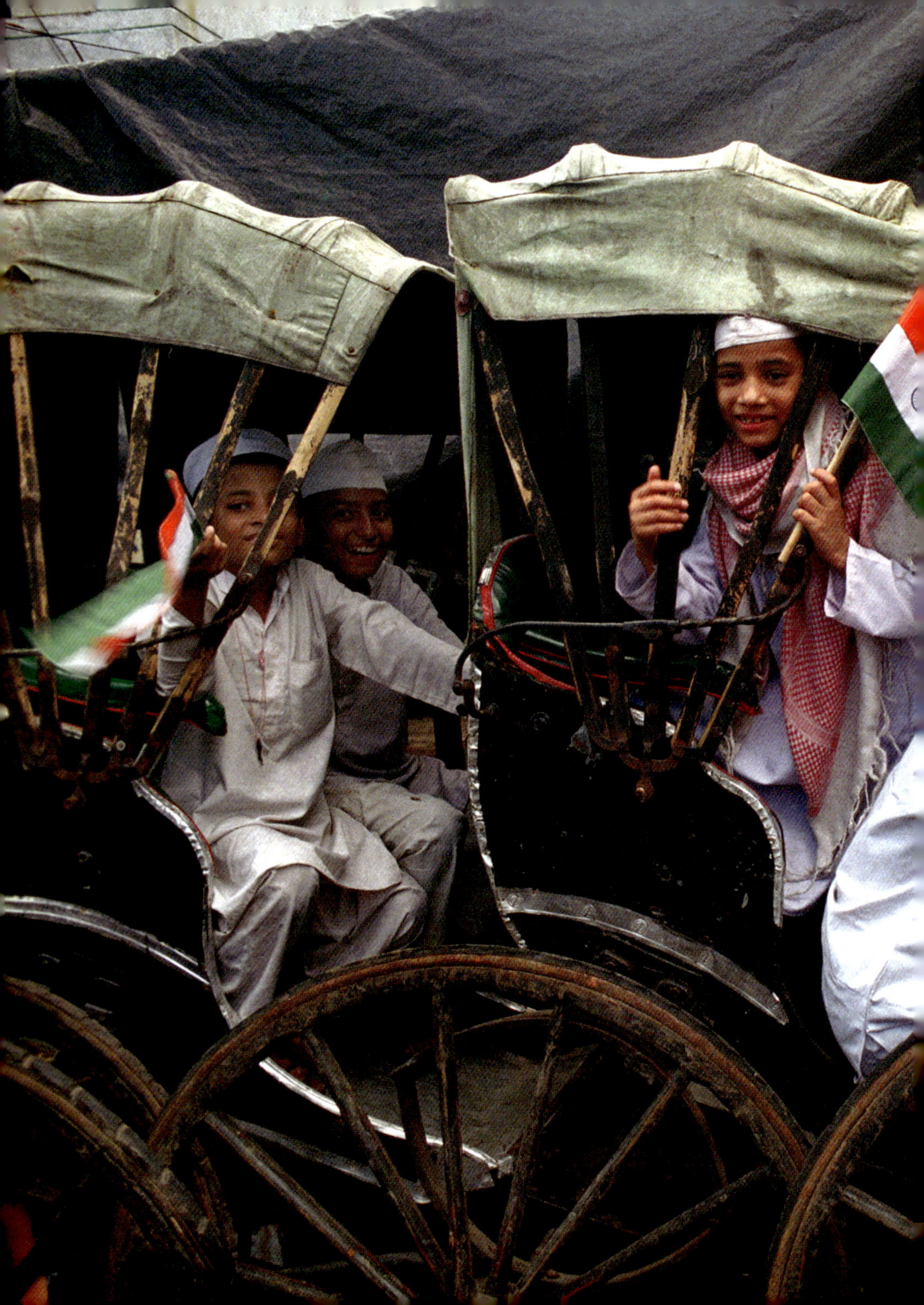

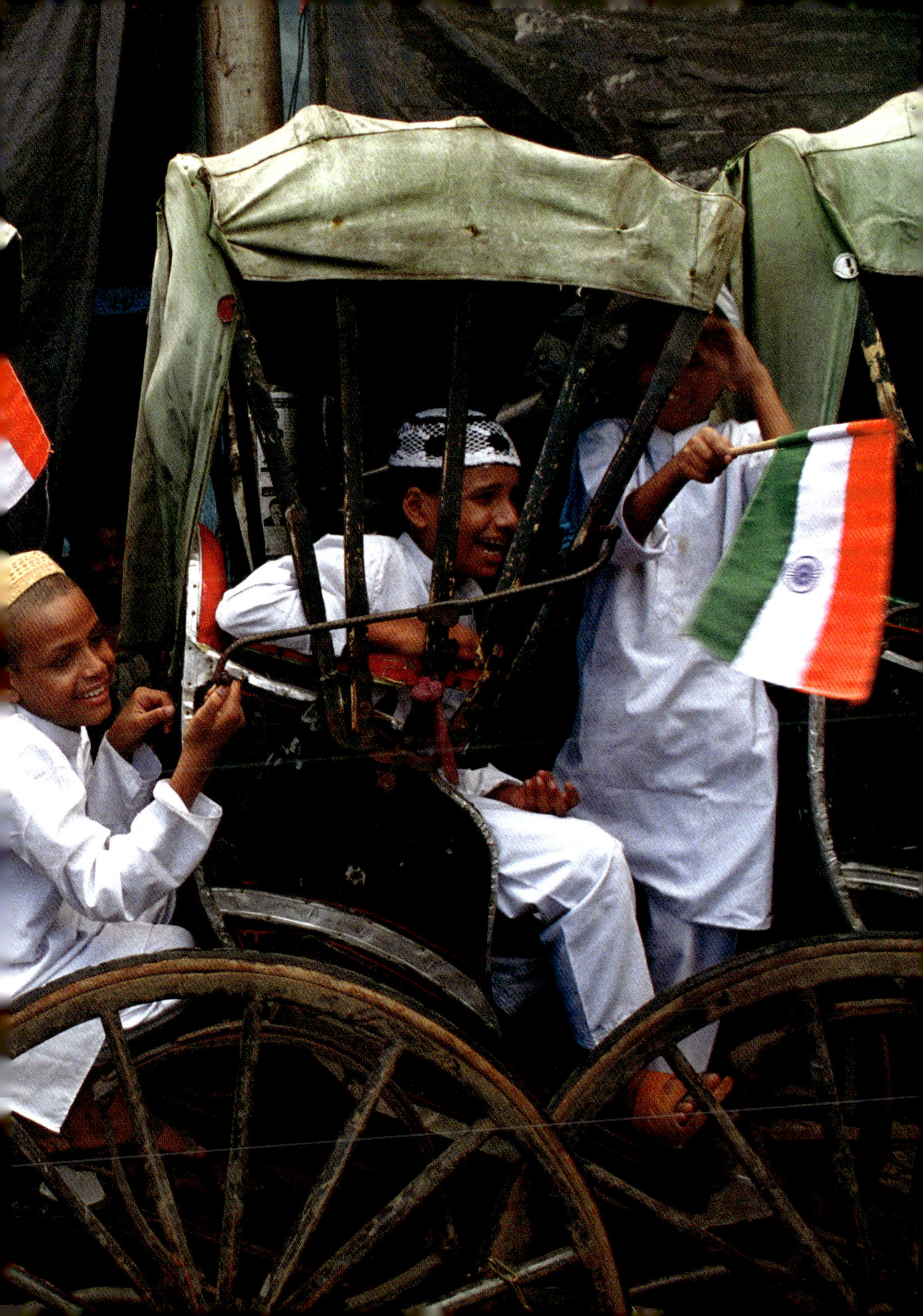

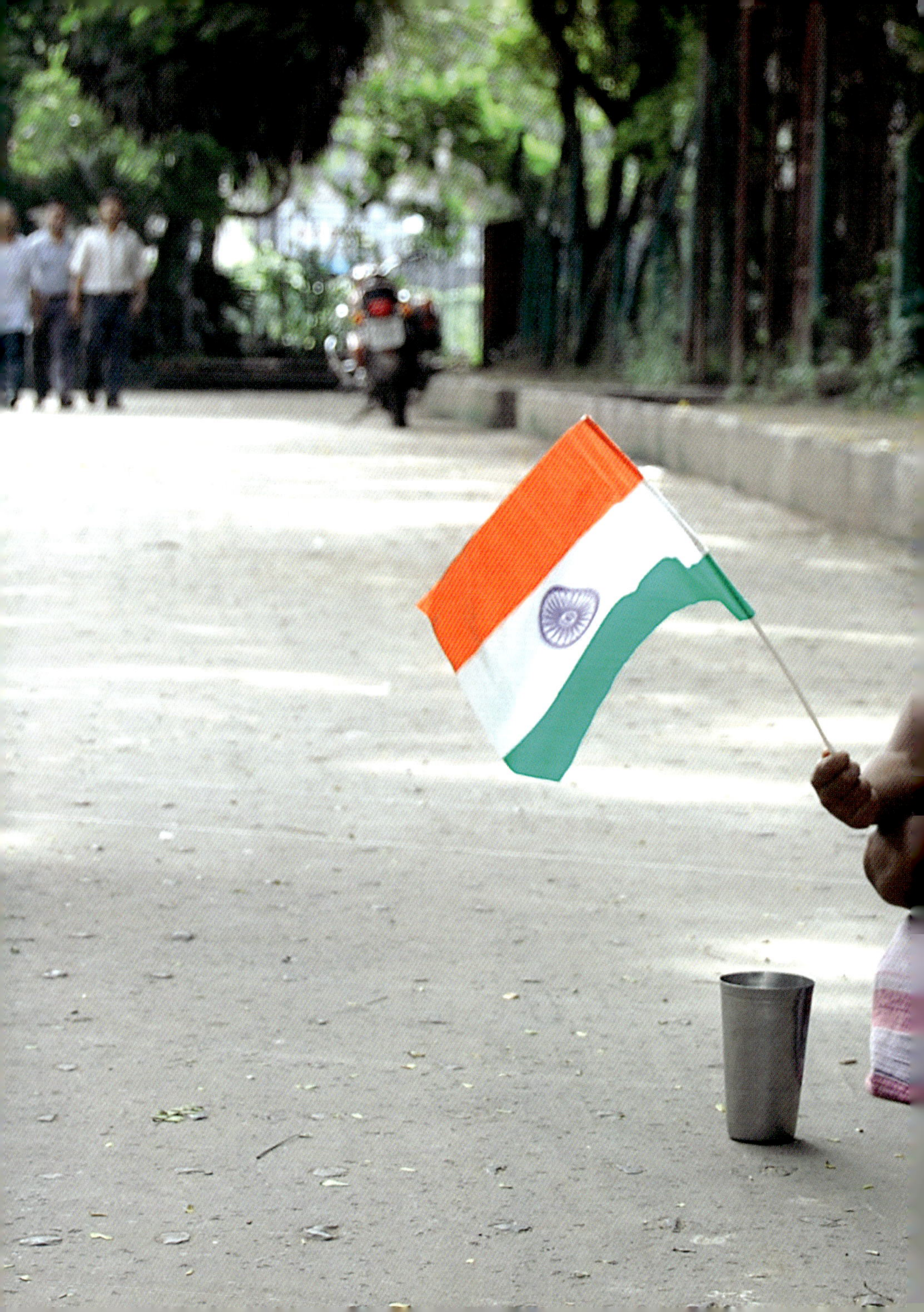

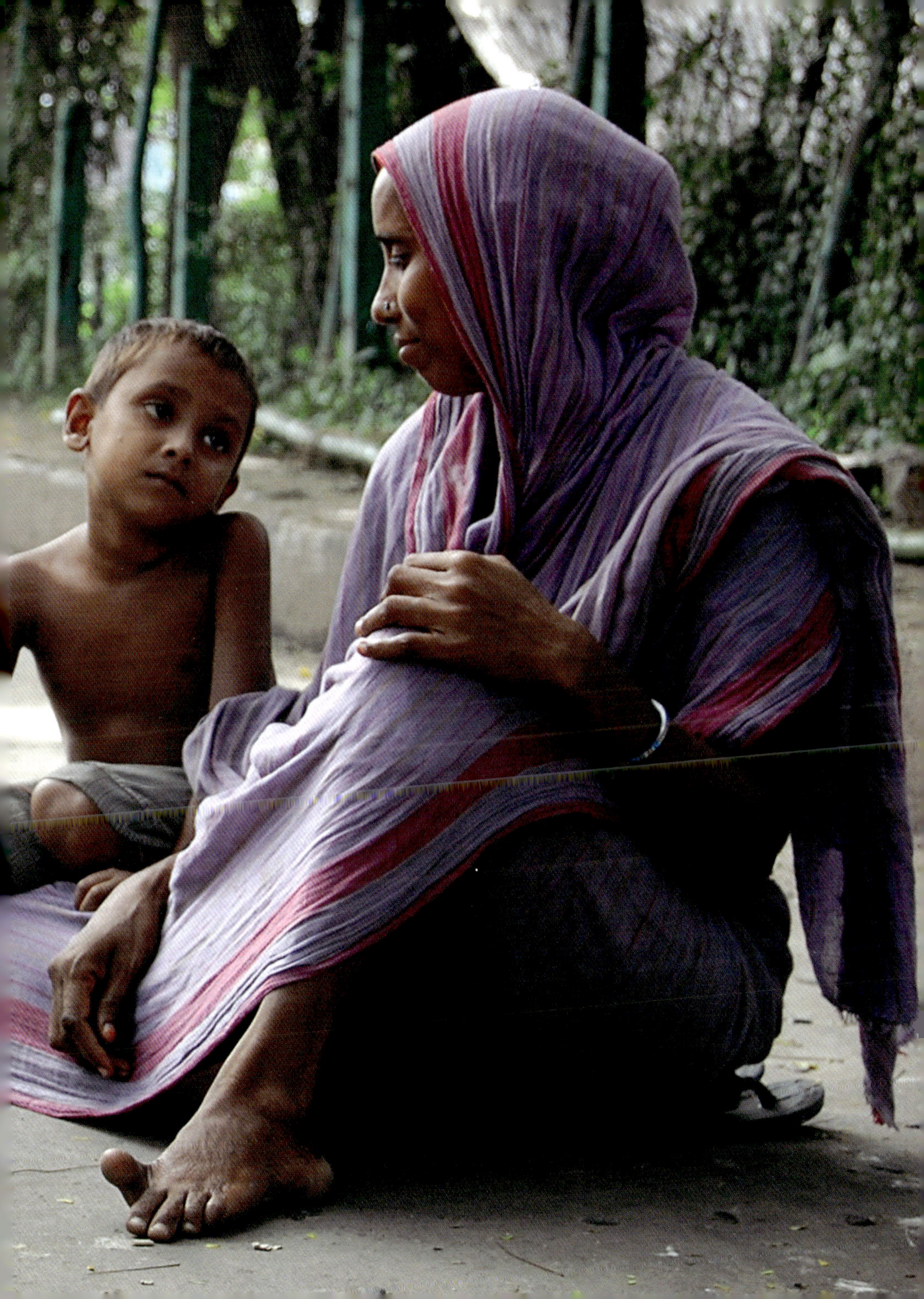

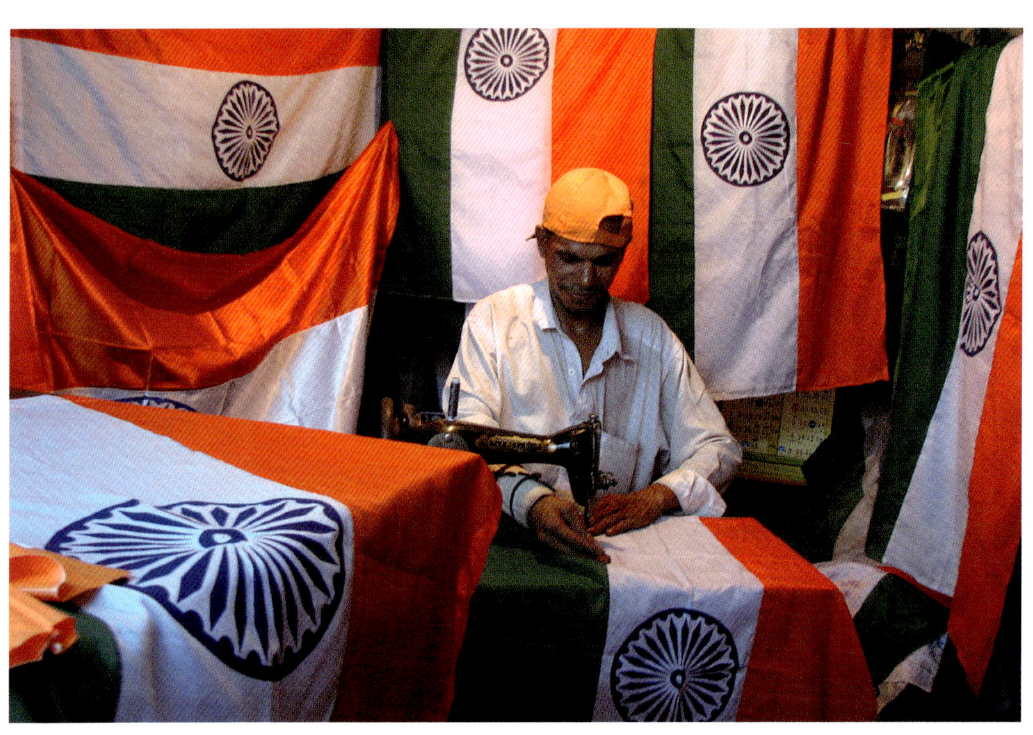

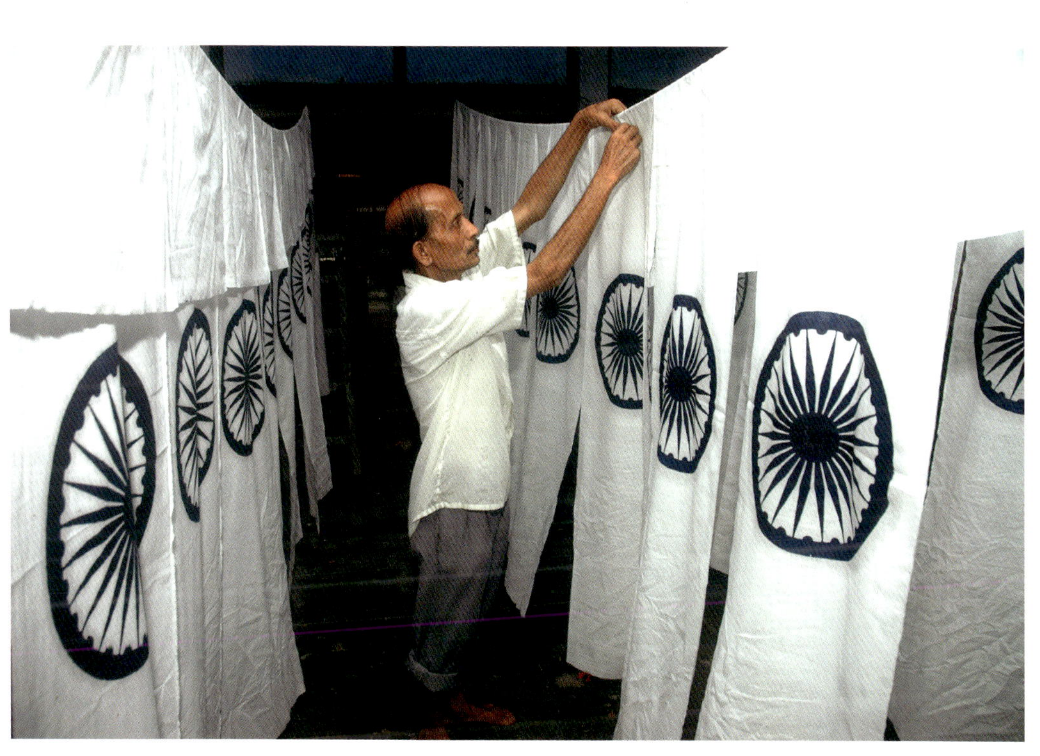

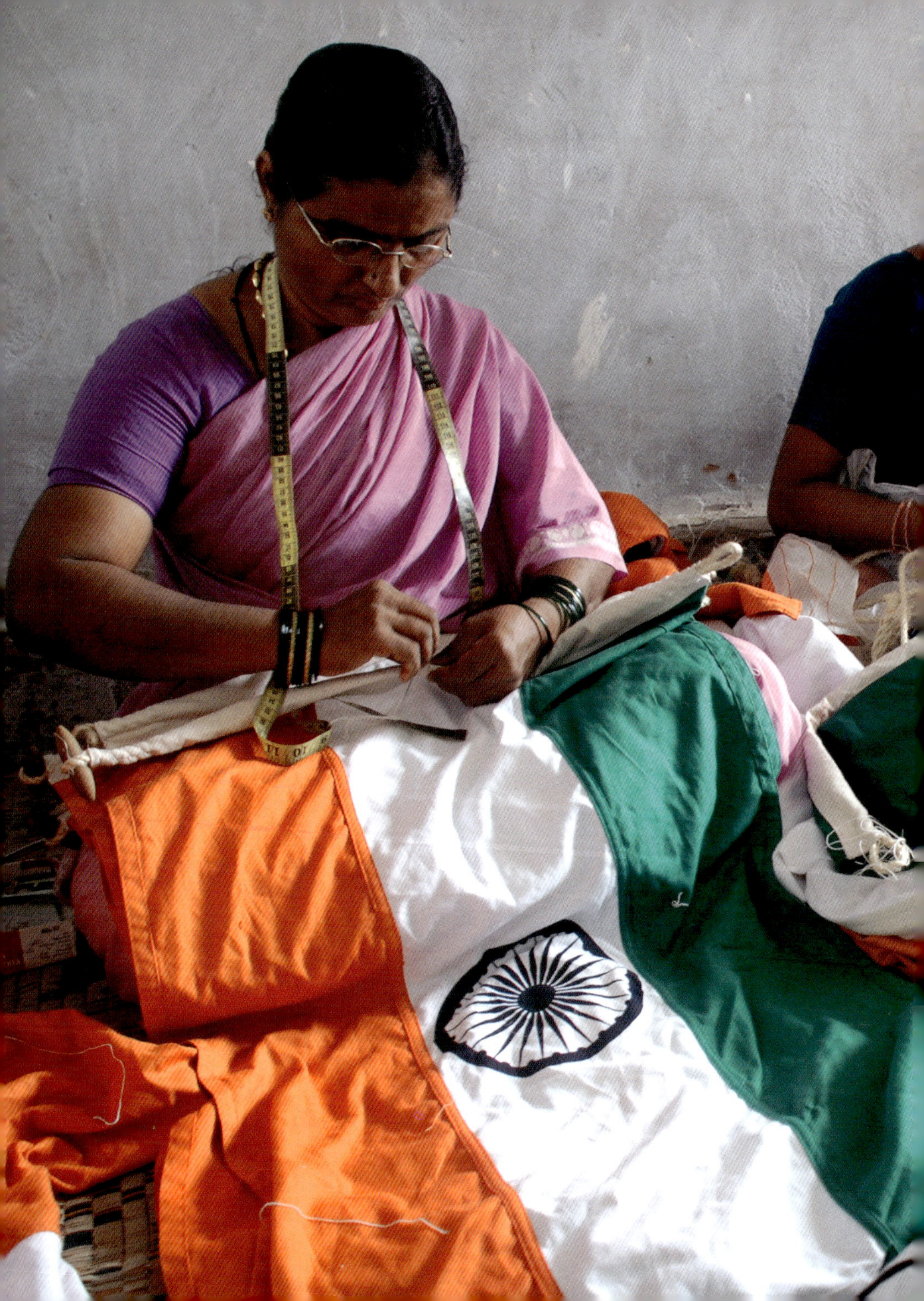

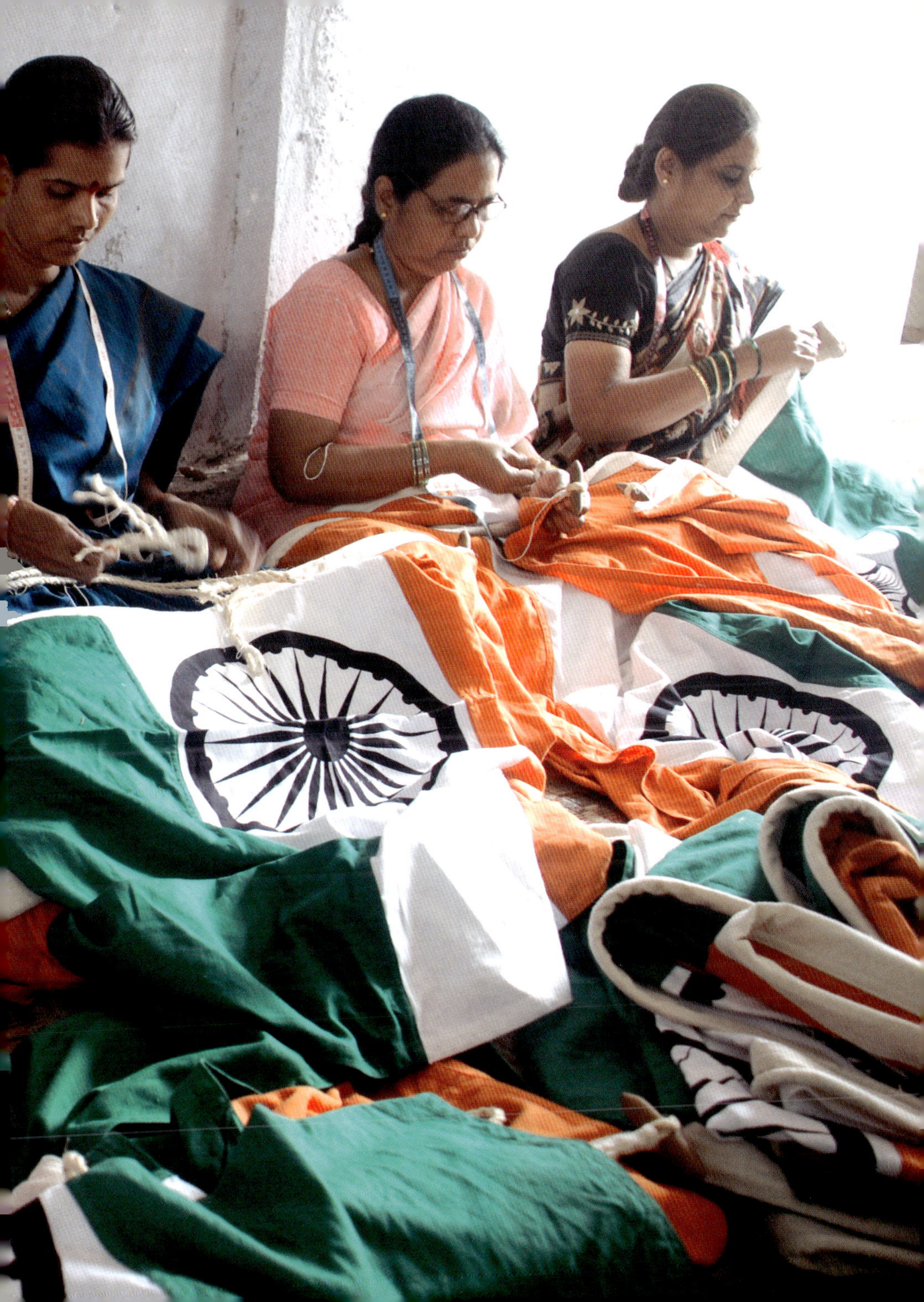

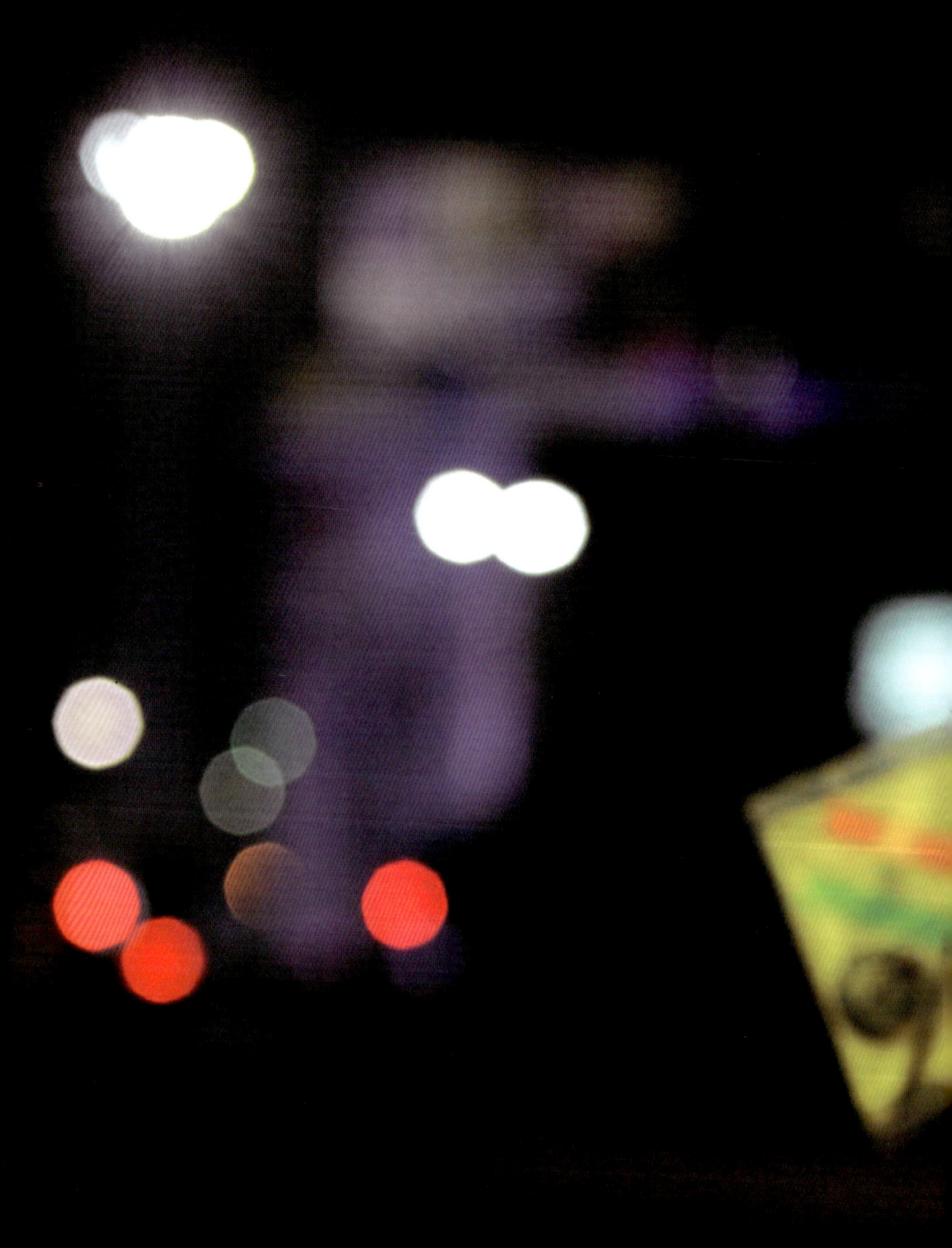

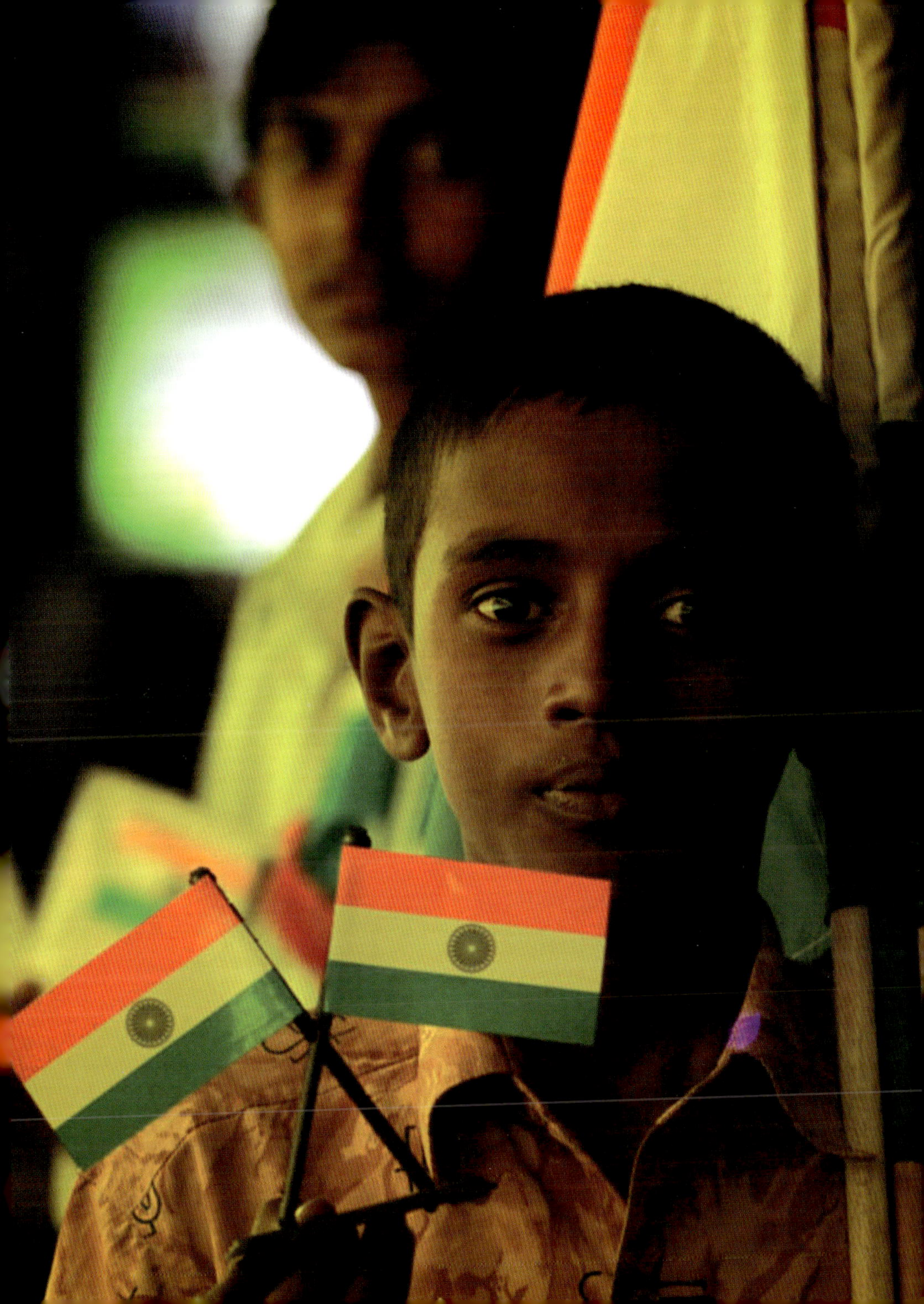

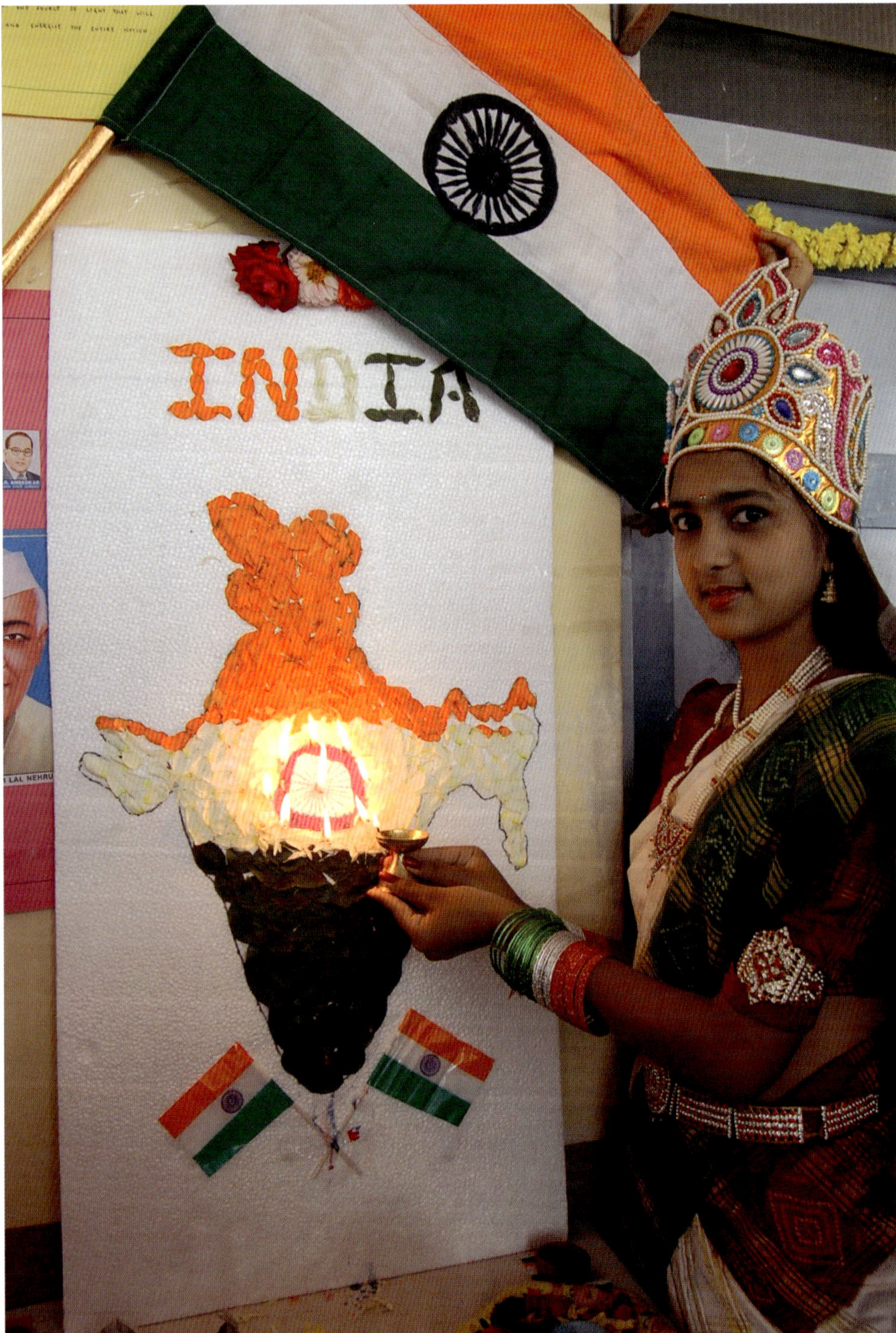
THE PEOPLE IS LIGHT THAT WILL
AND CHERLIE THE ENTIRE NATION
B. AMBEDKAR
LAL NEHRU
INDIA

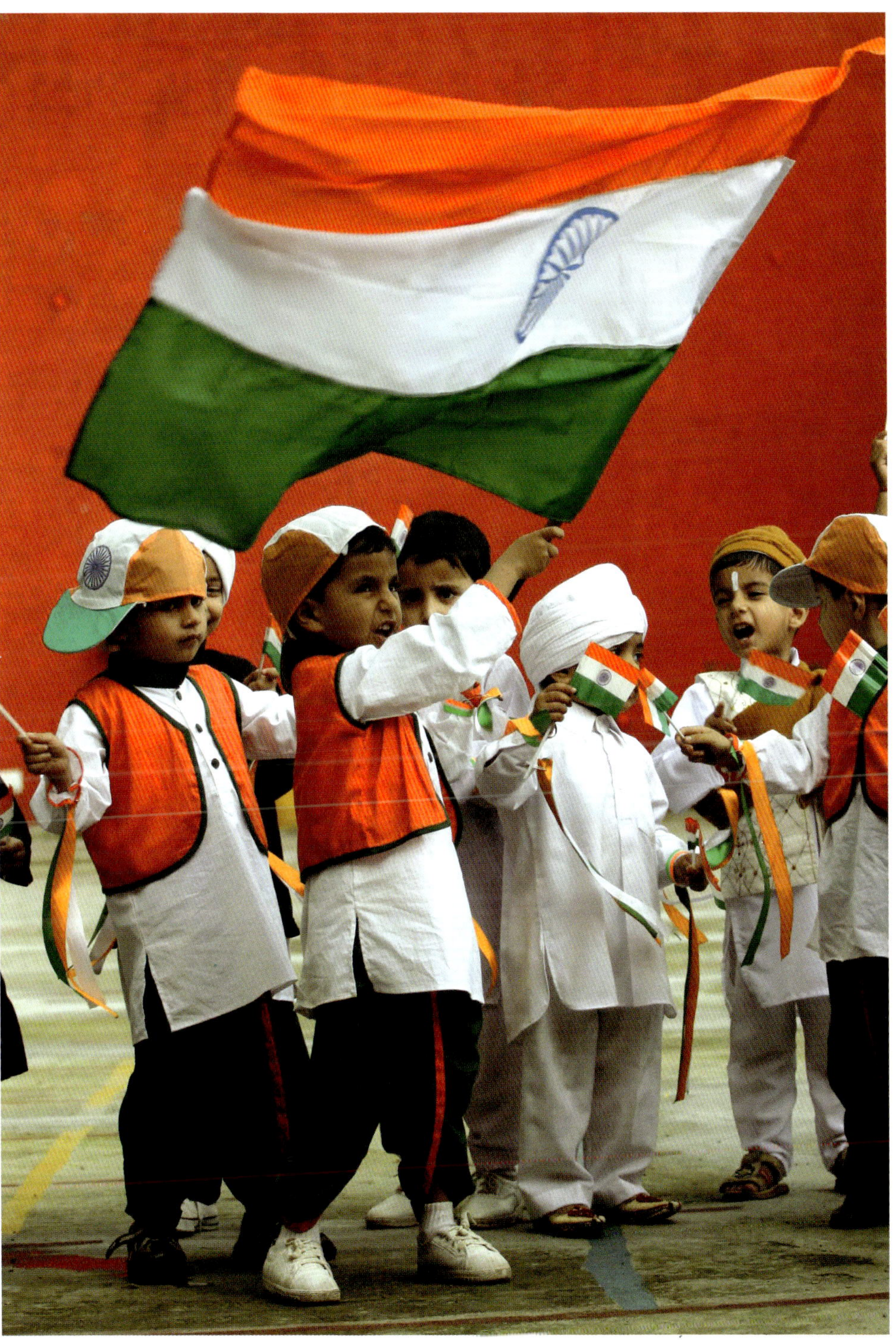

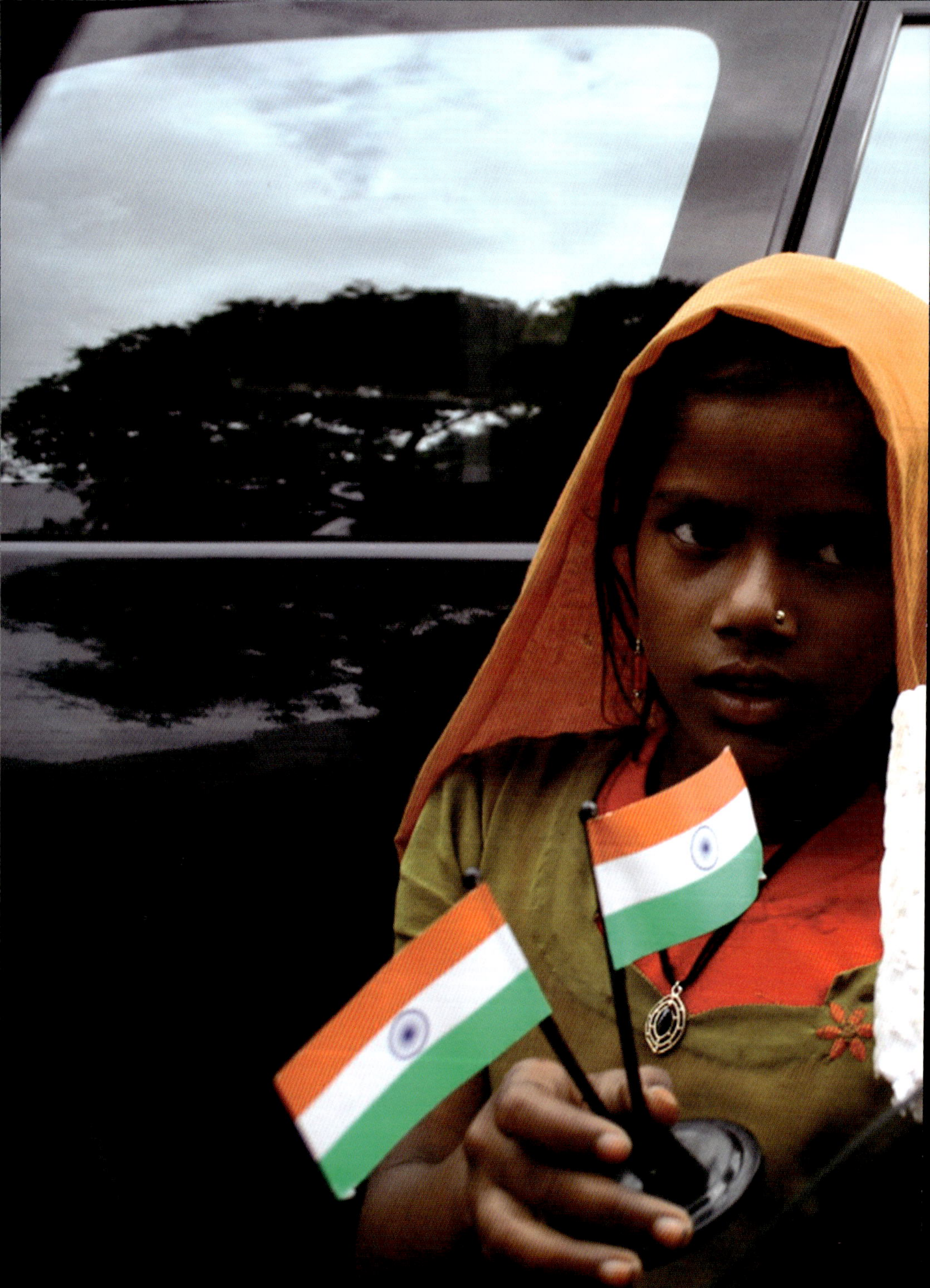

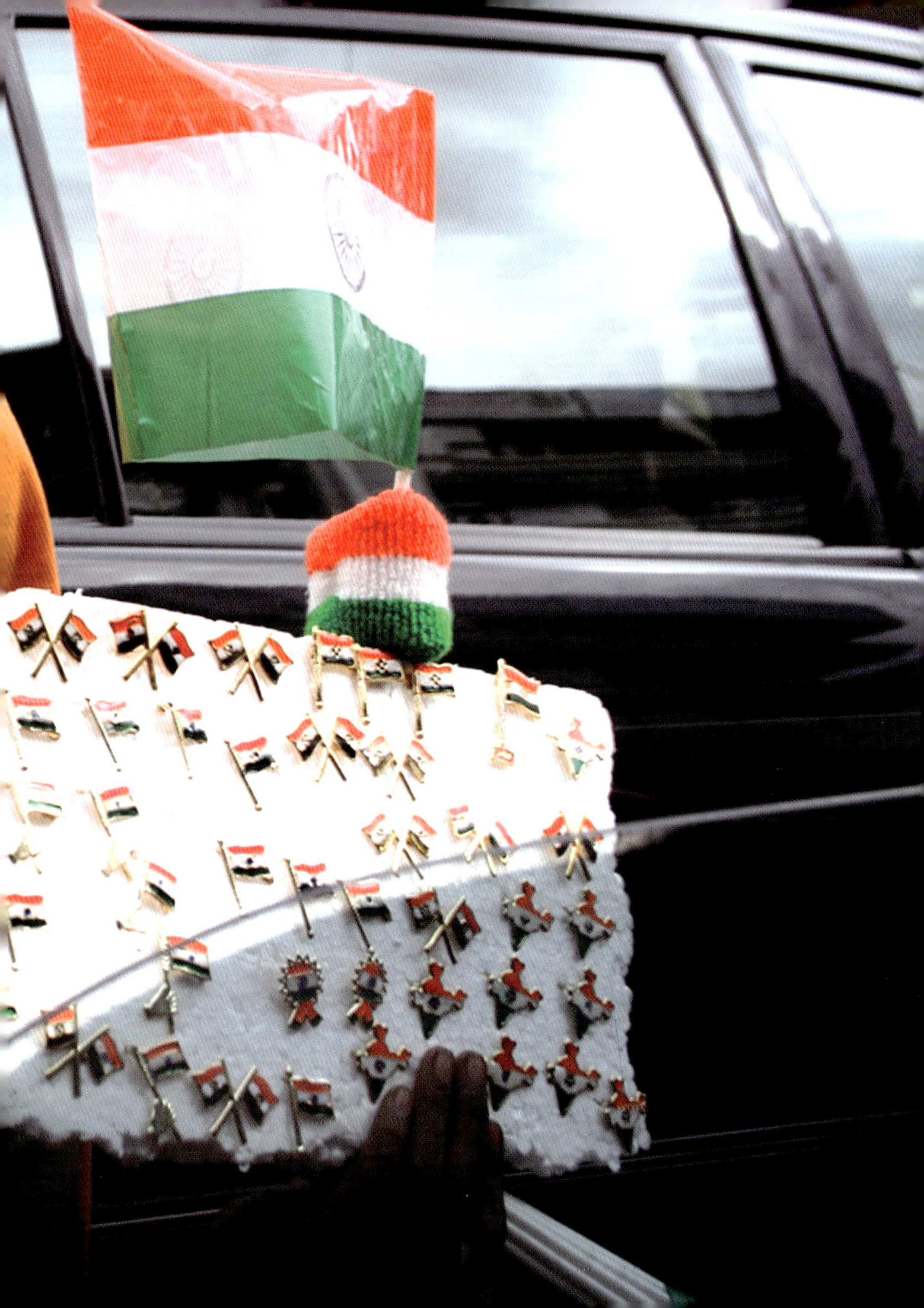

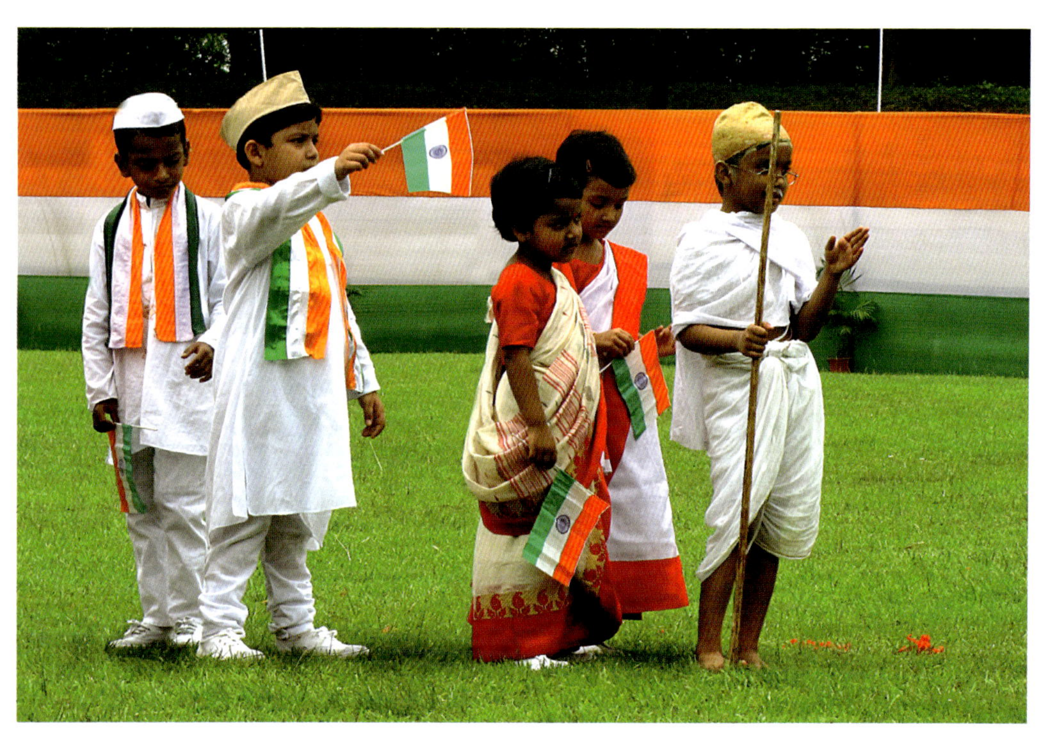

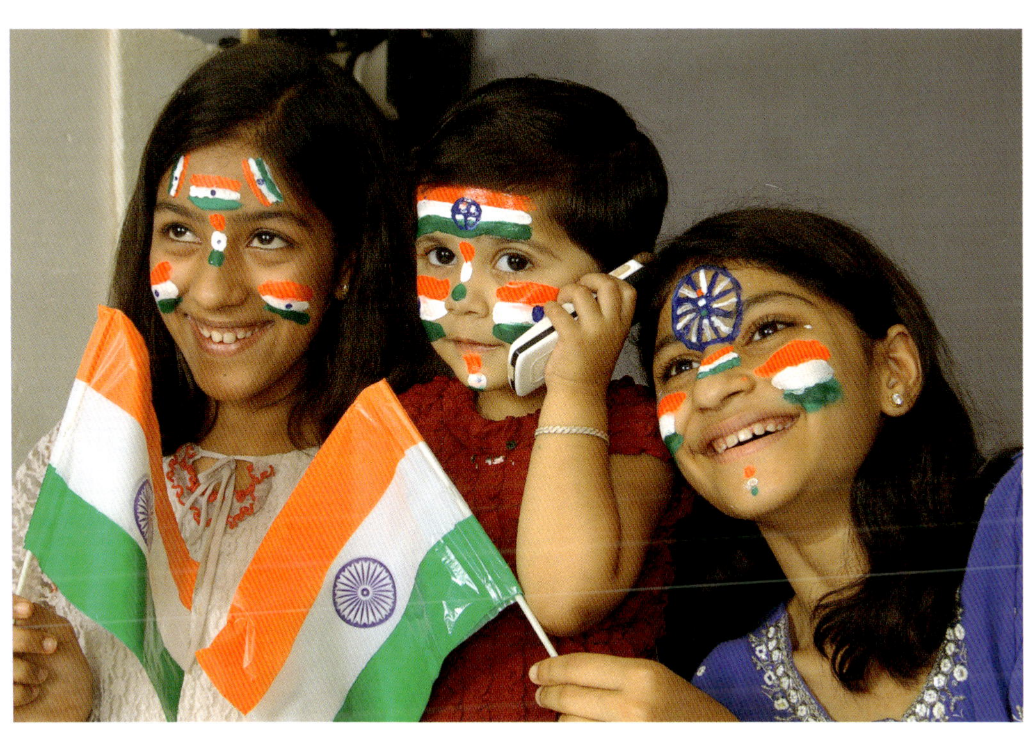

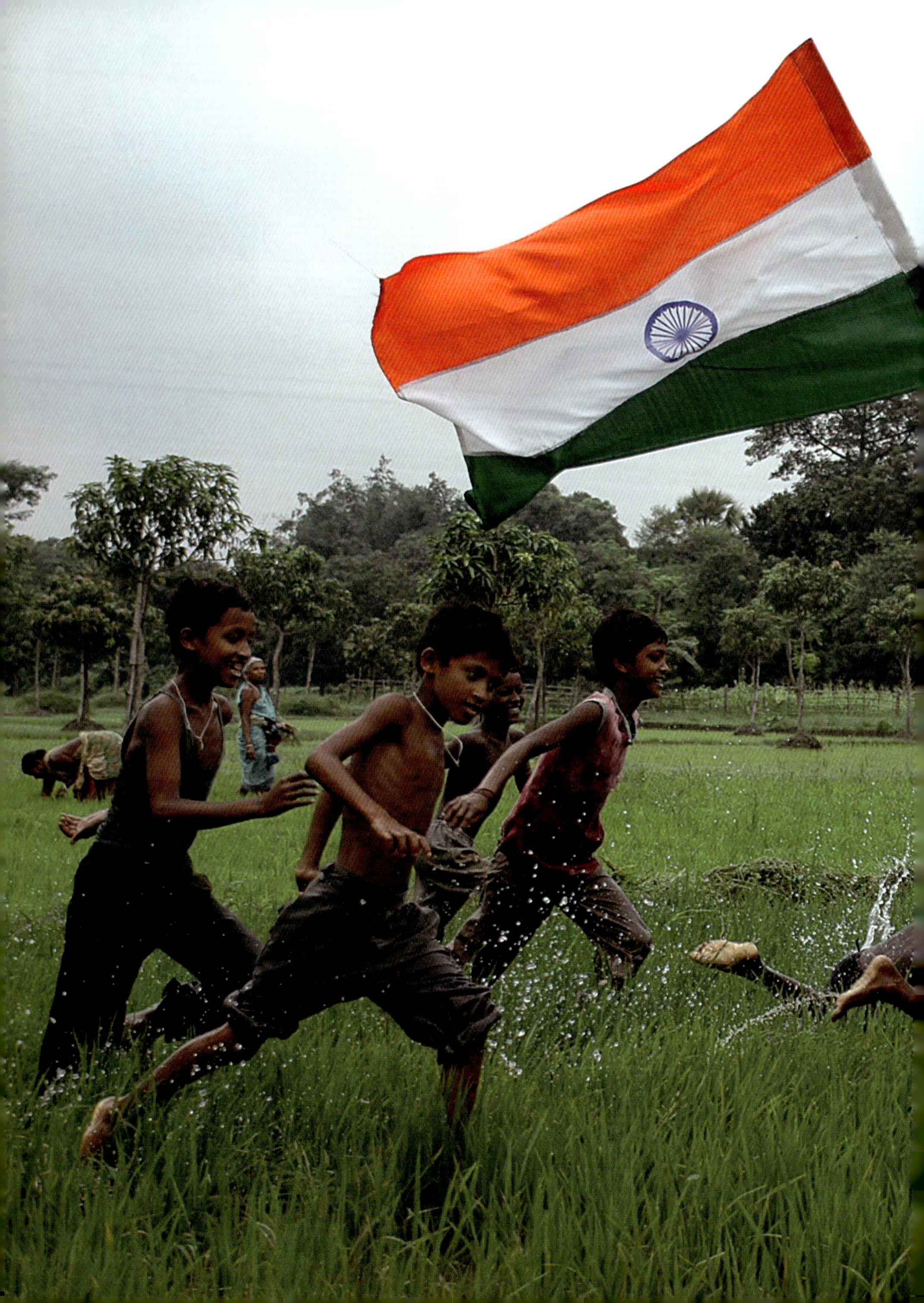

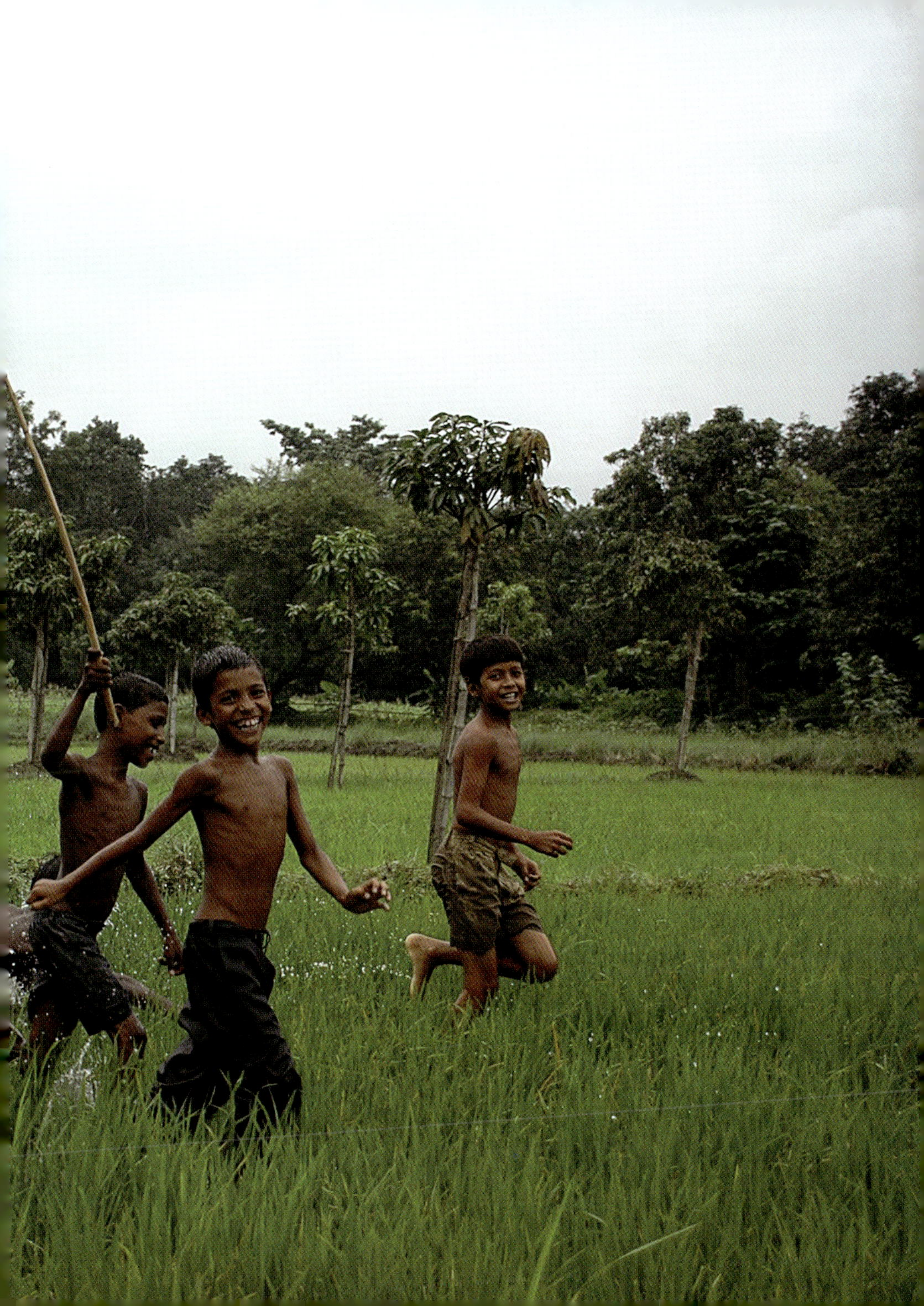

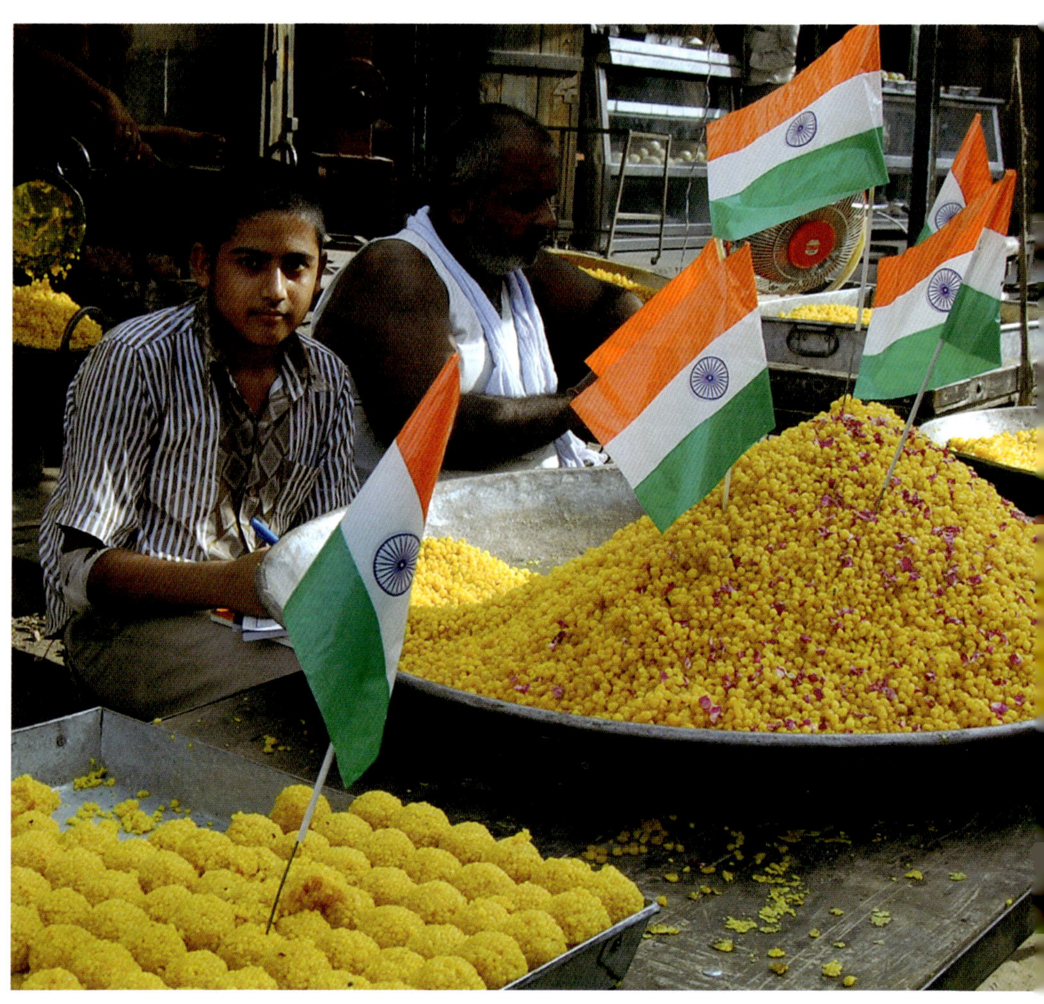

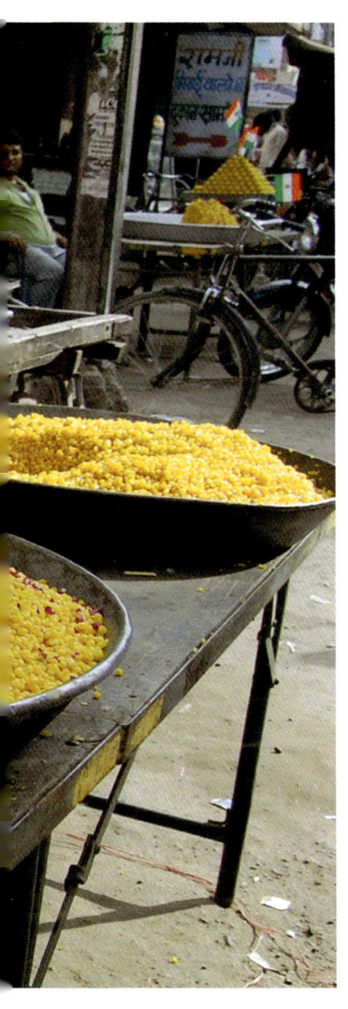

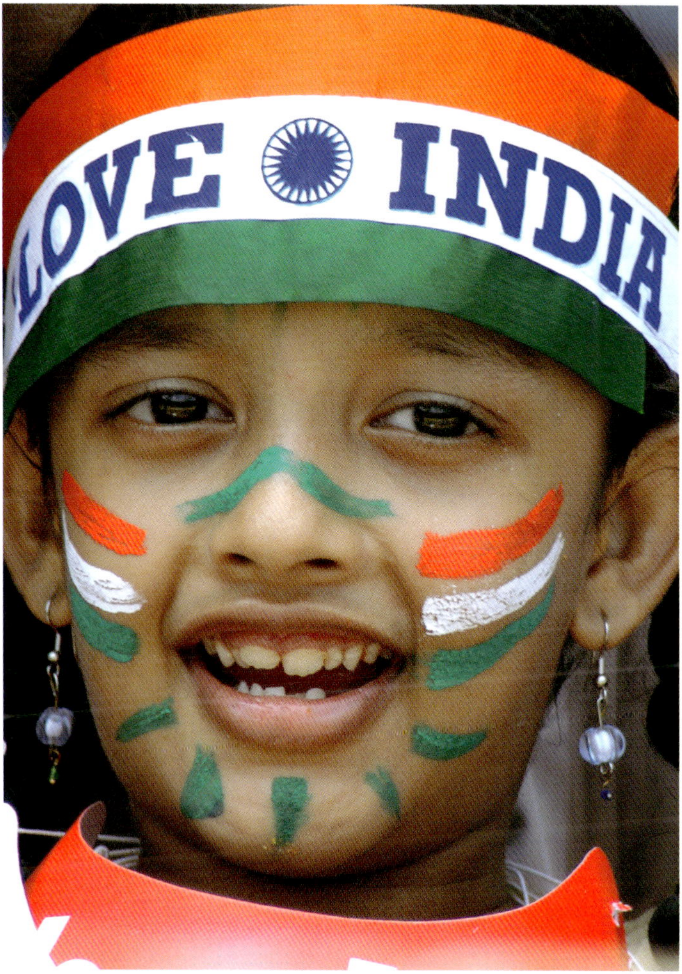

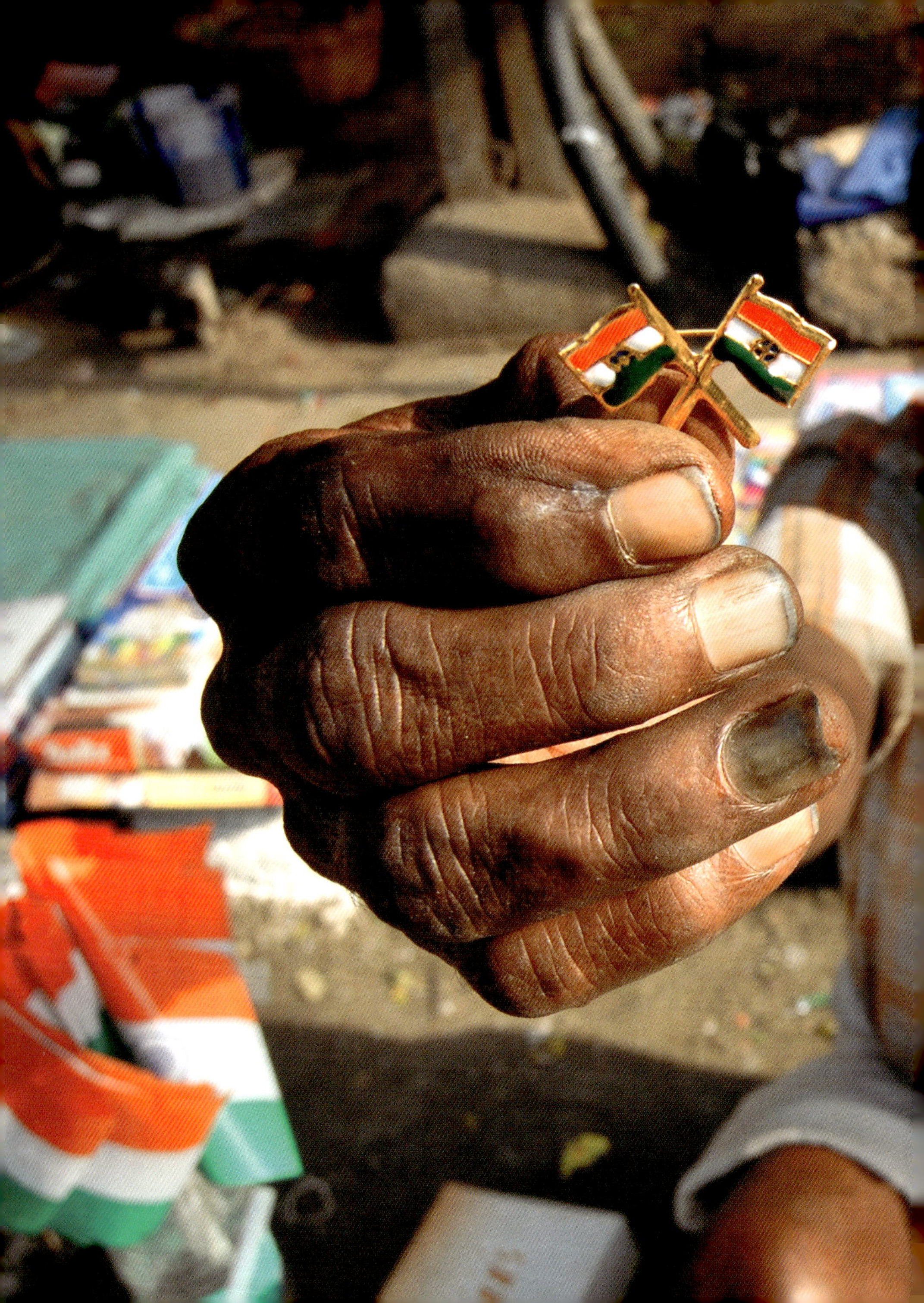

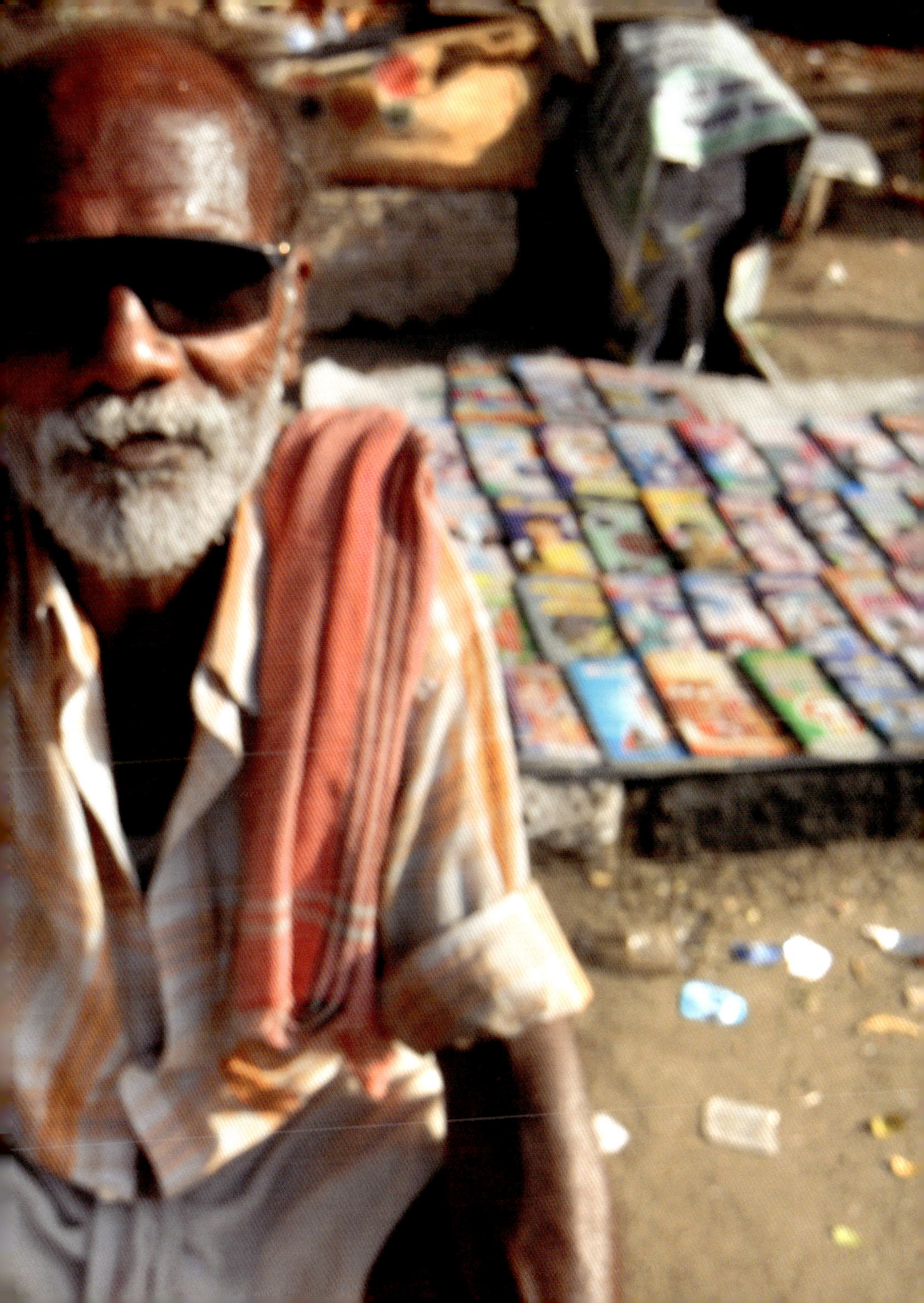

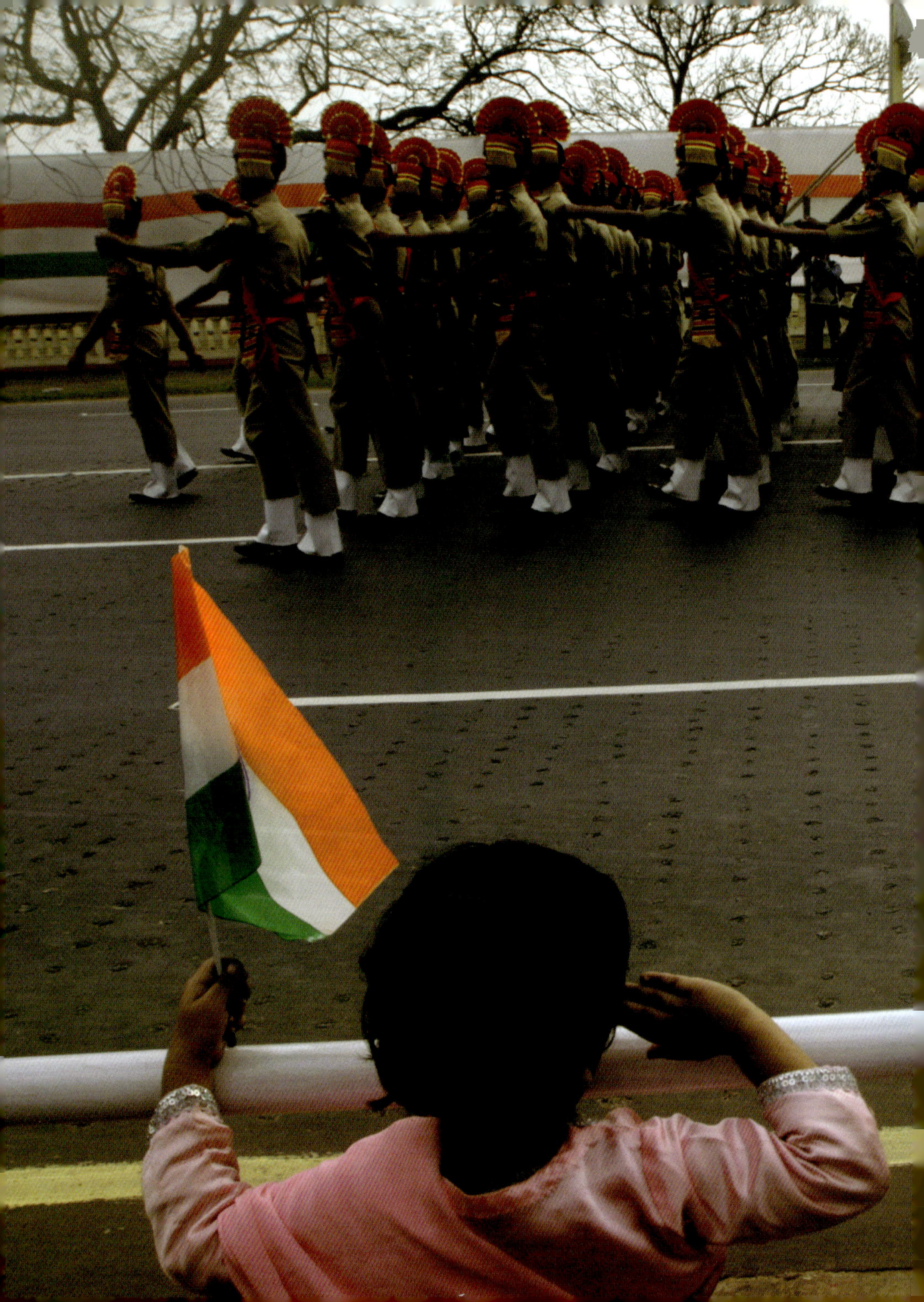

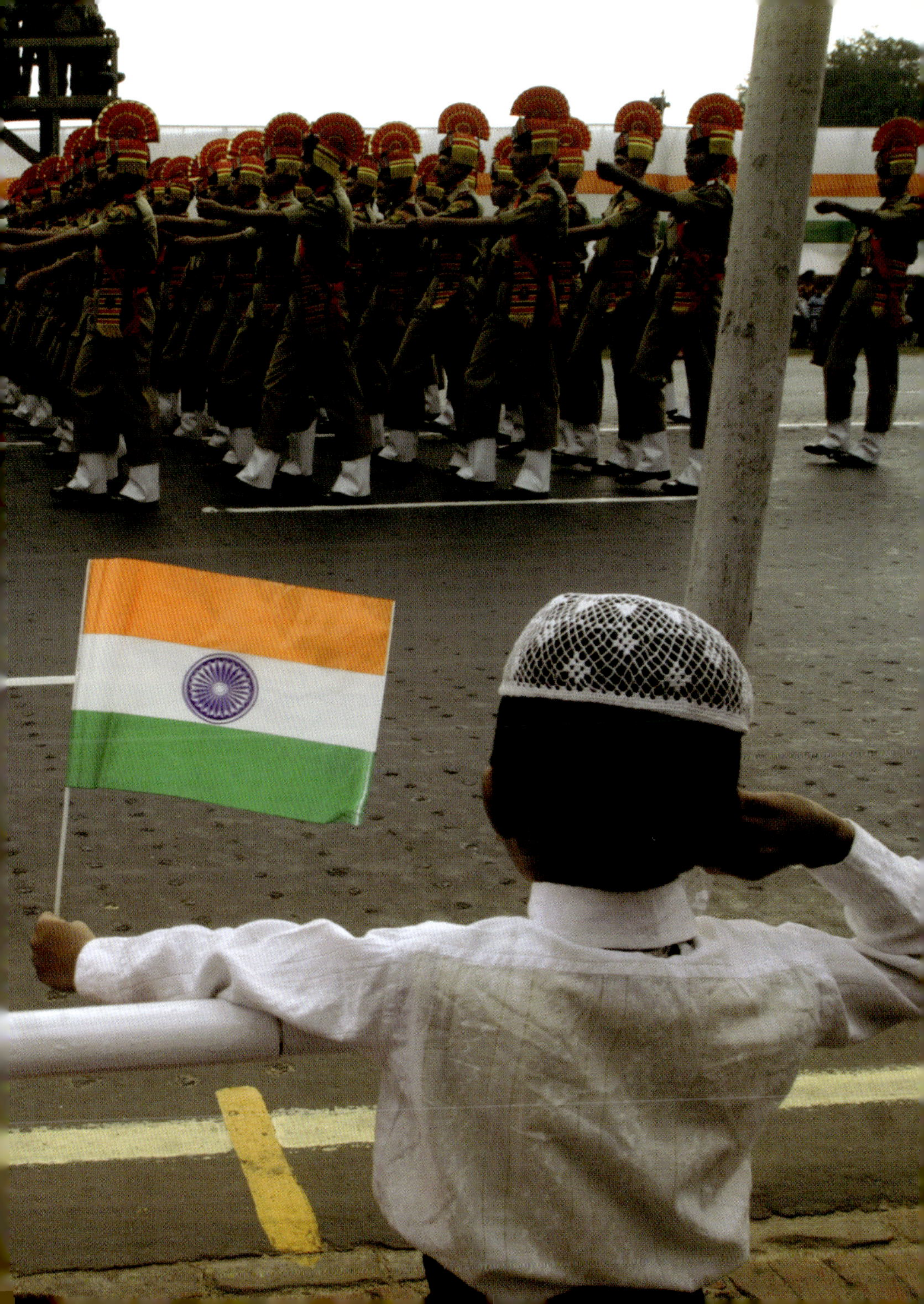

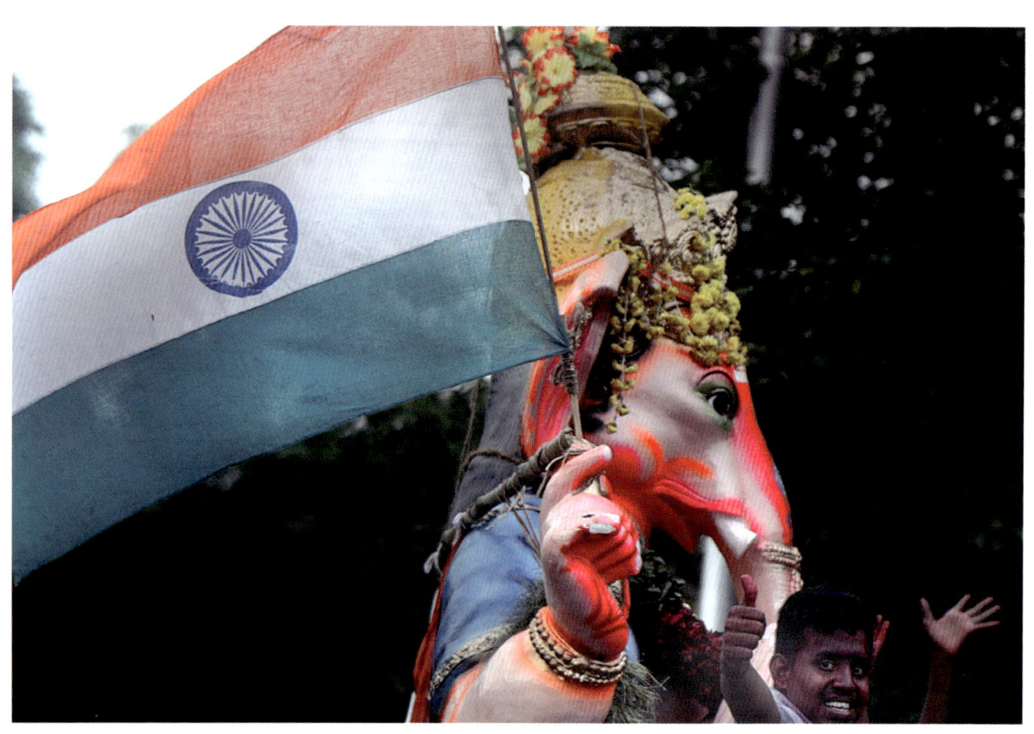

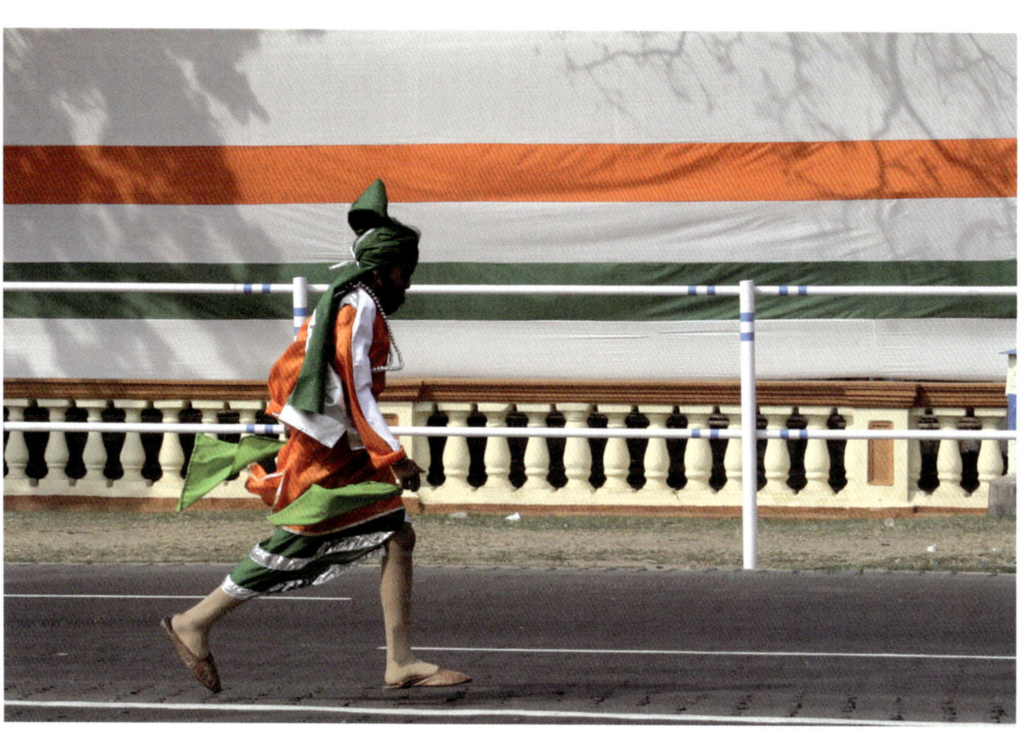

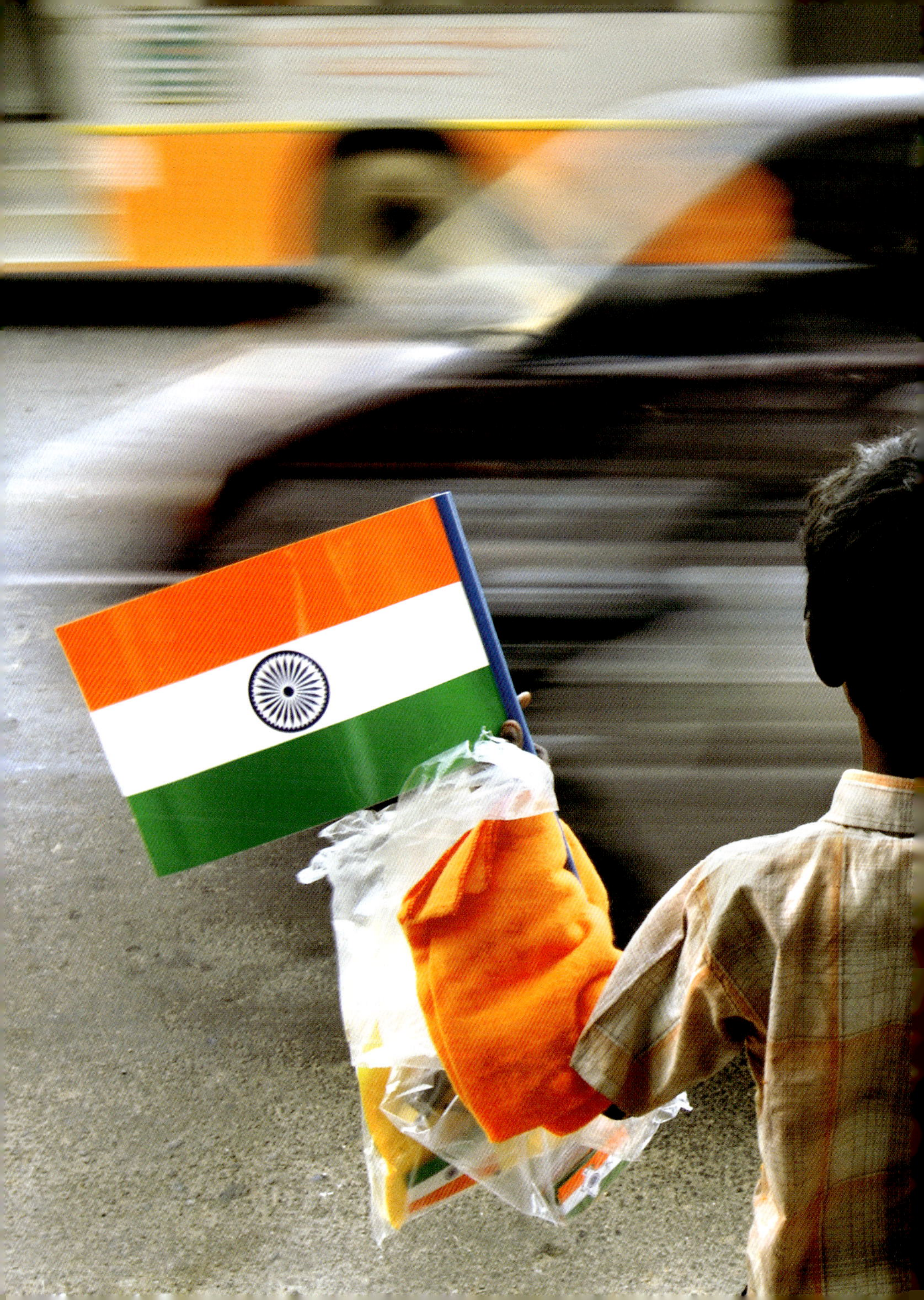

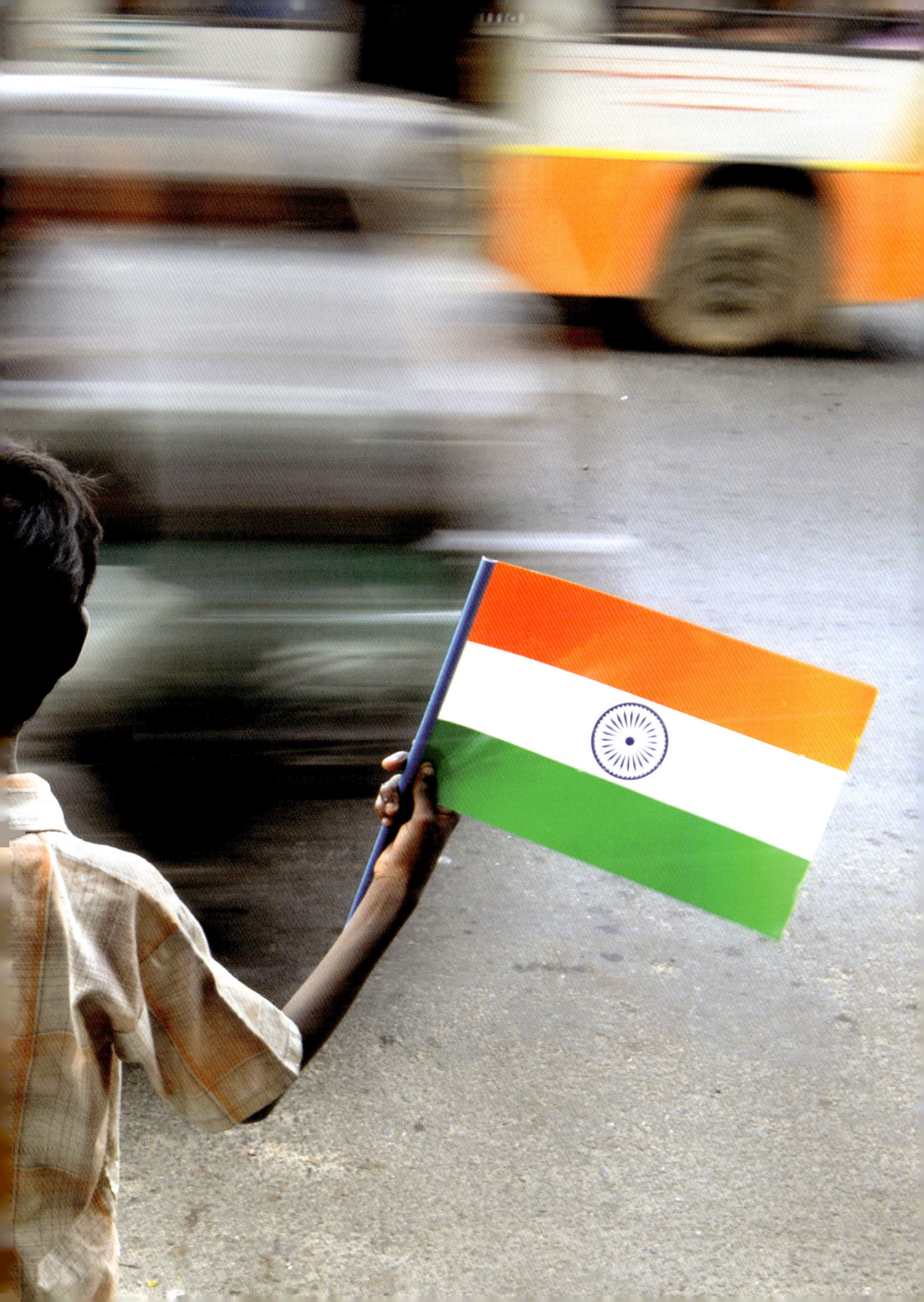

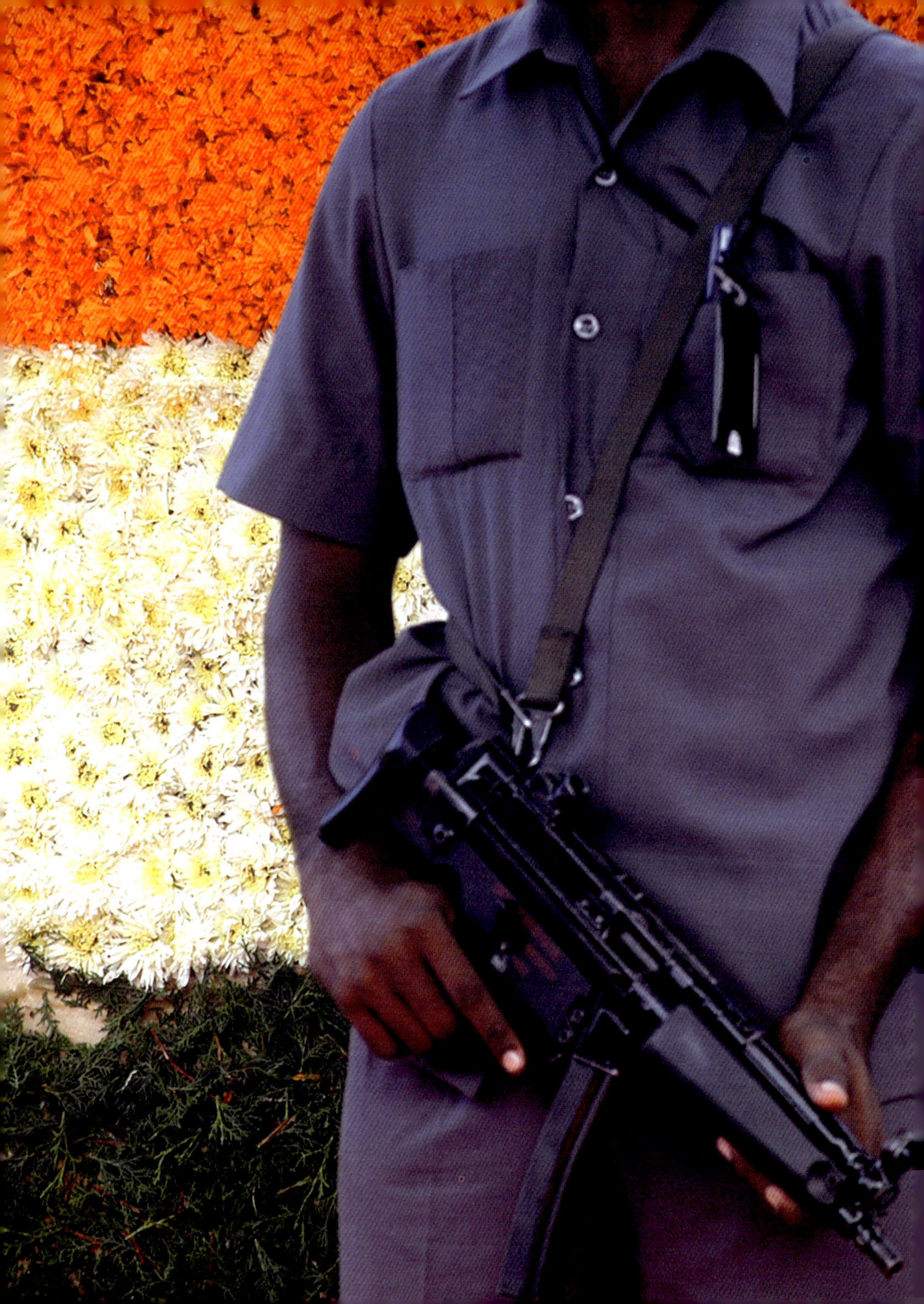

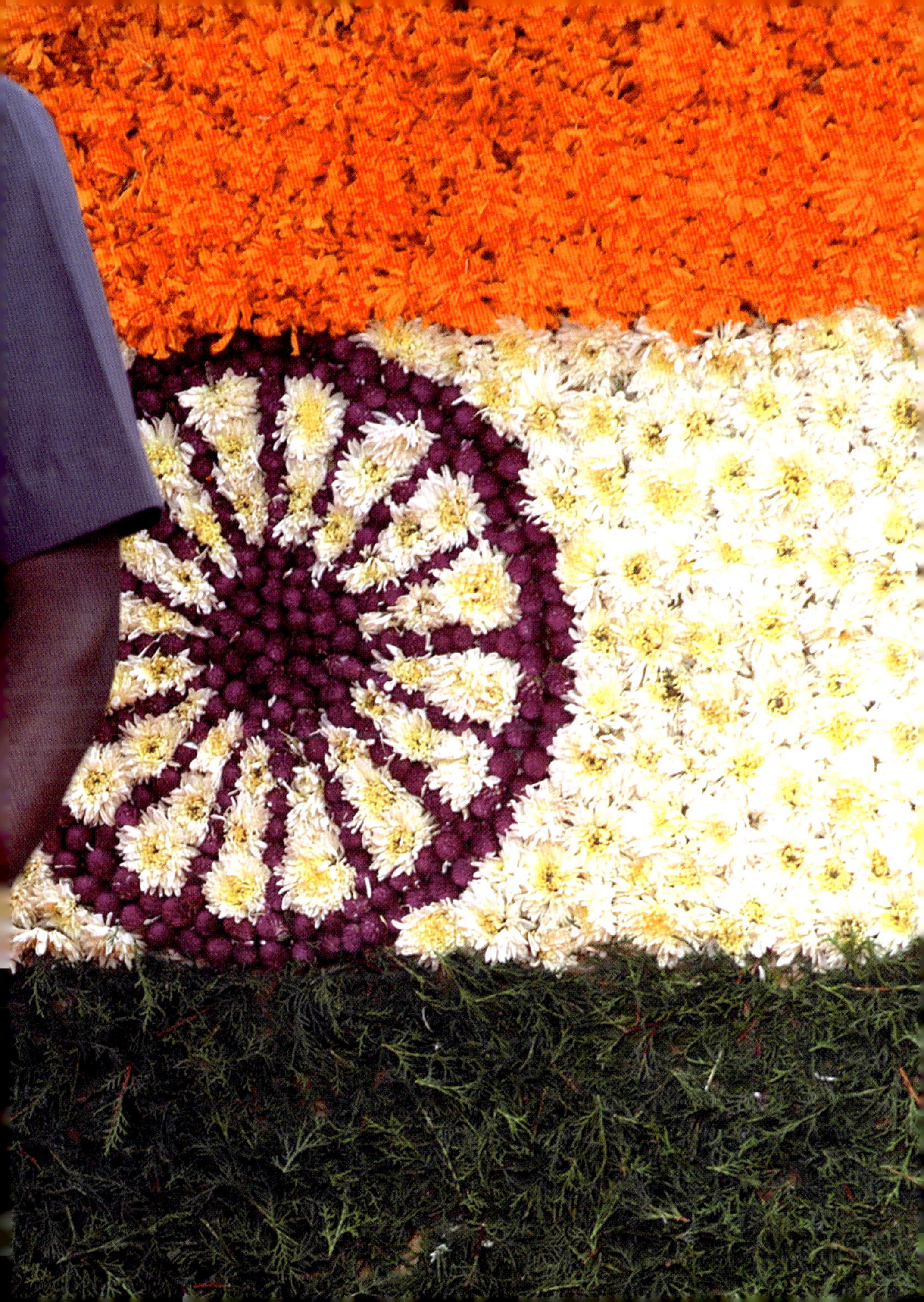

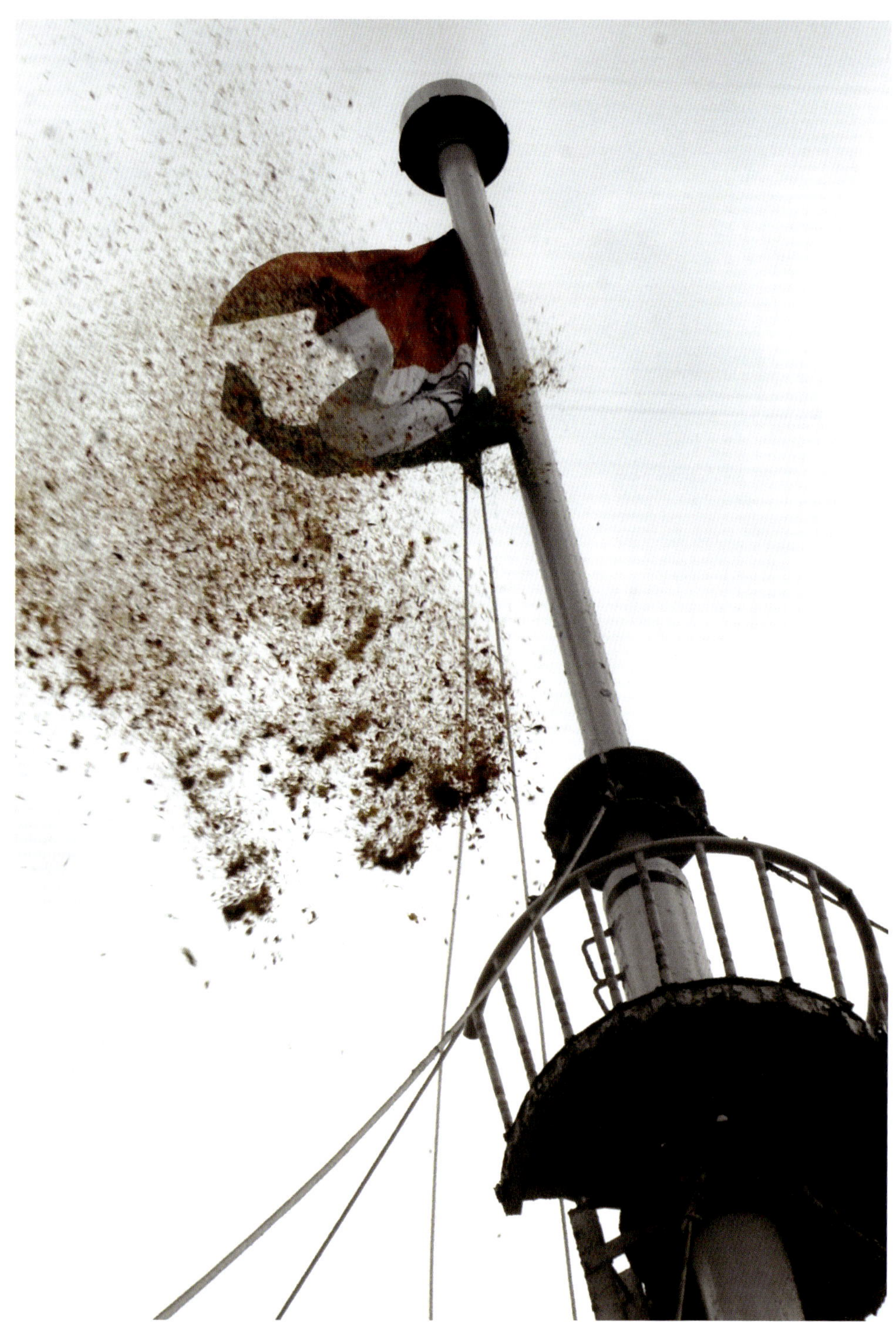

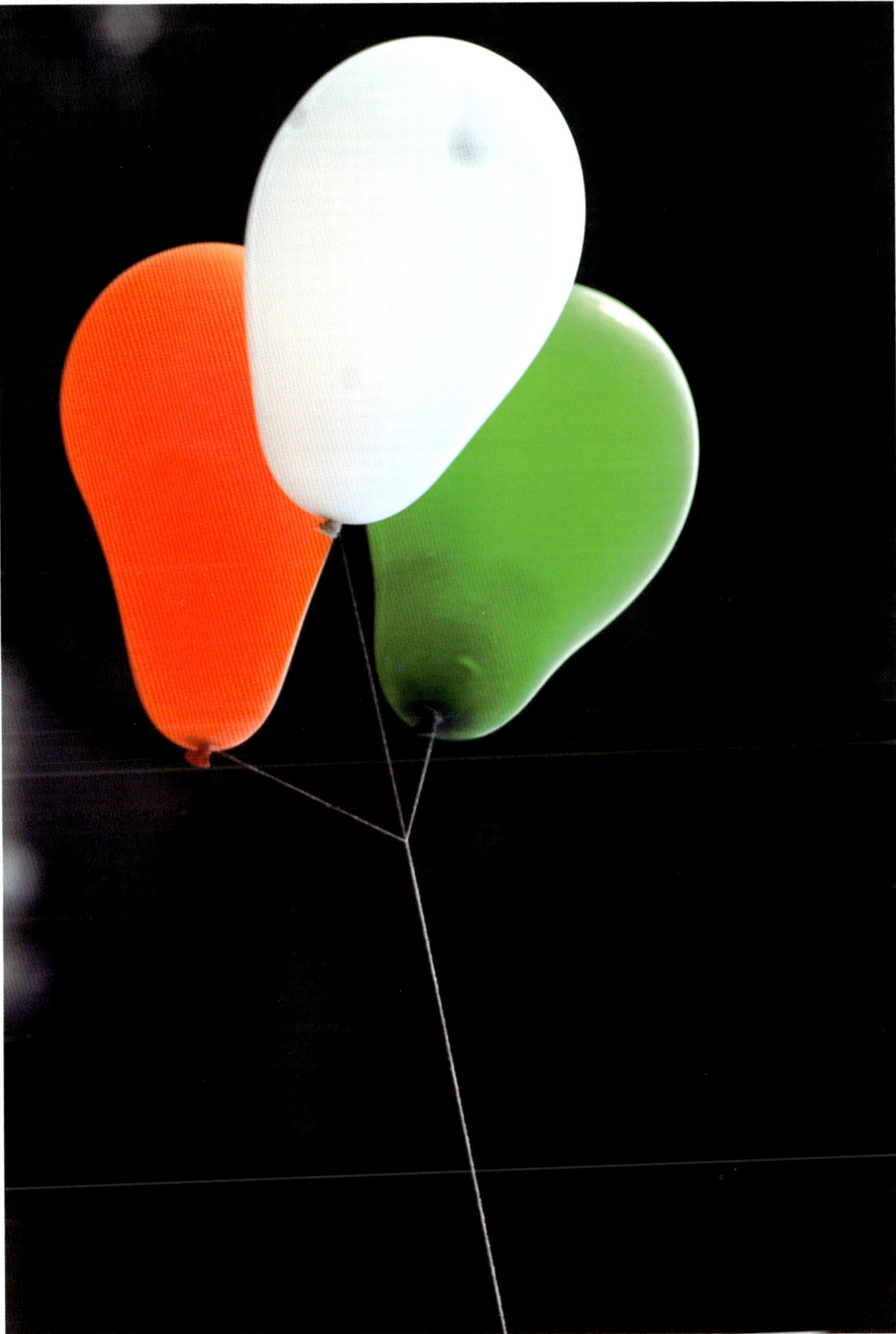

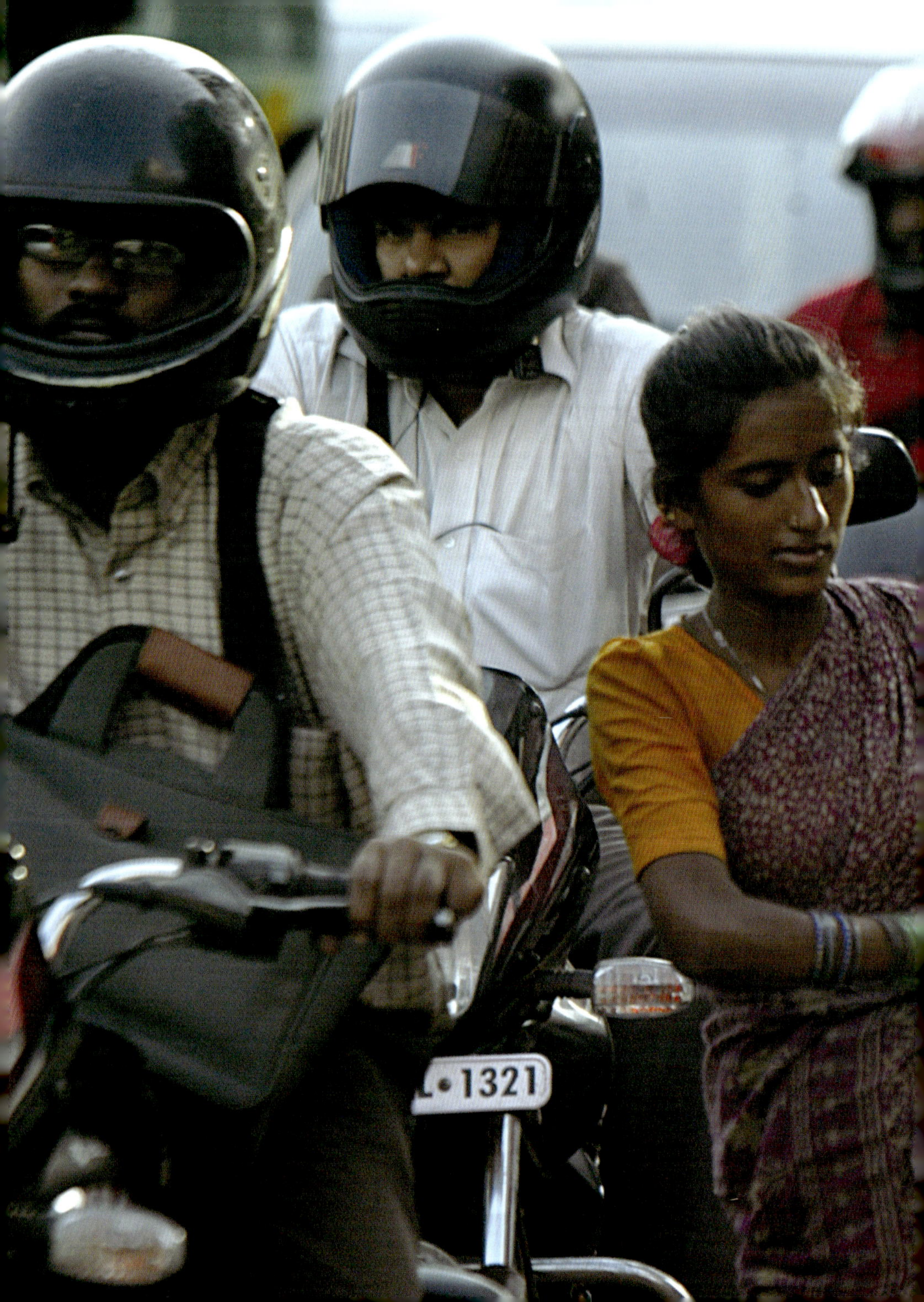

1321

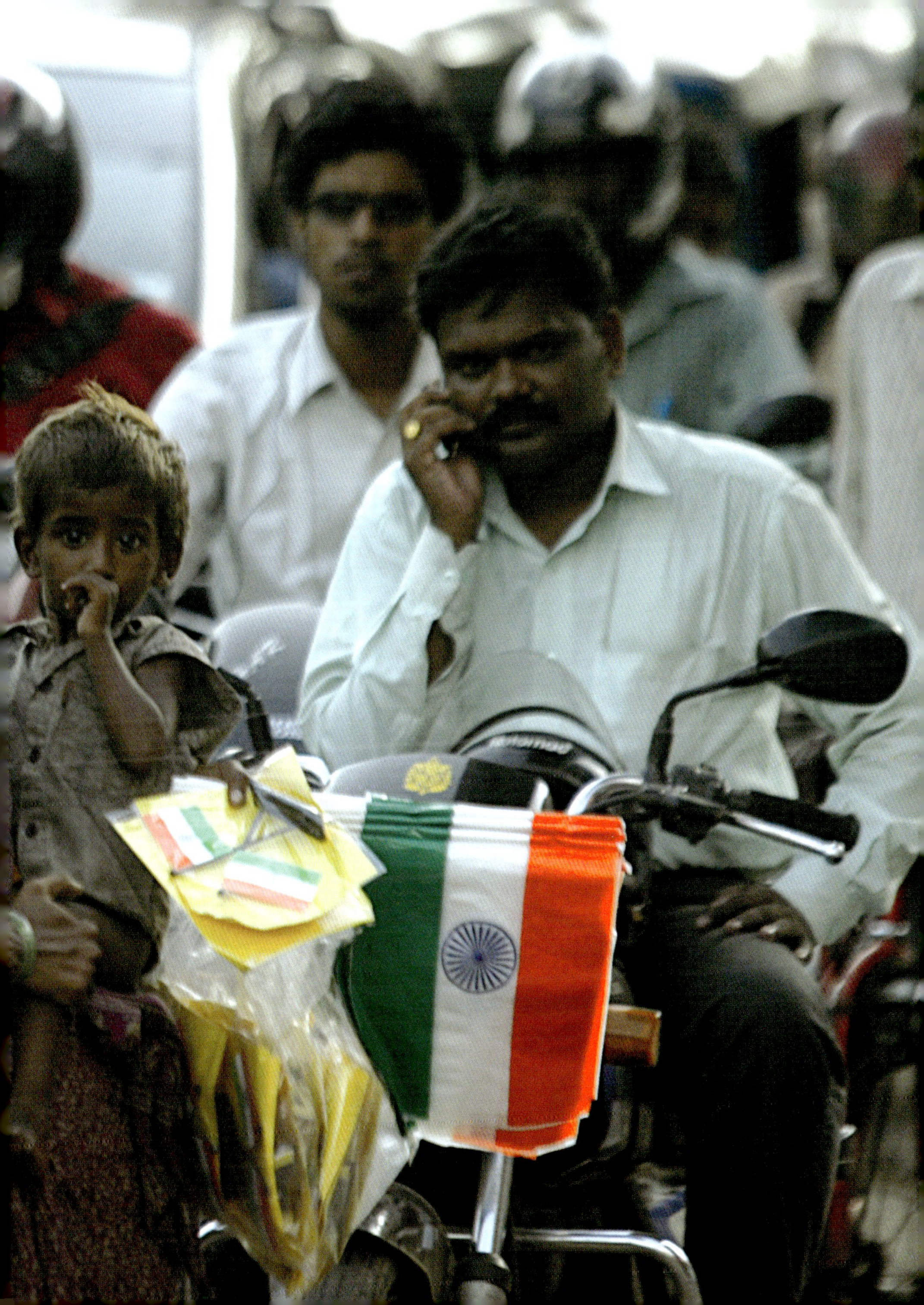

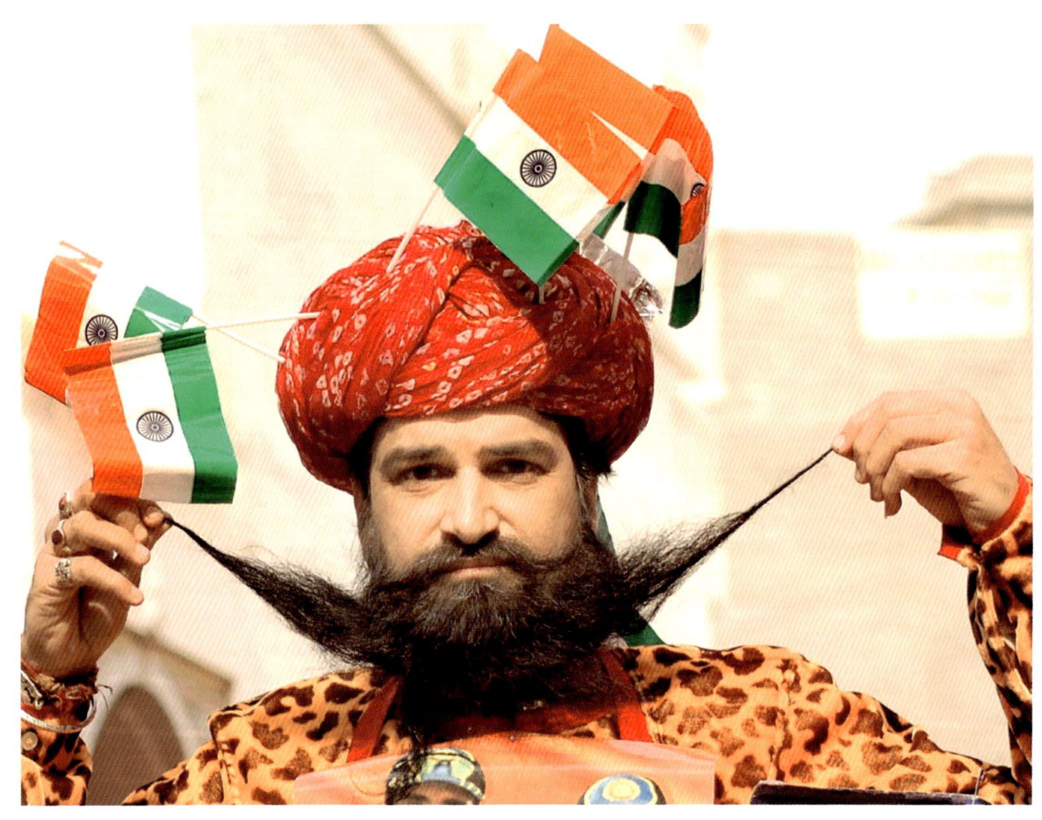

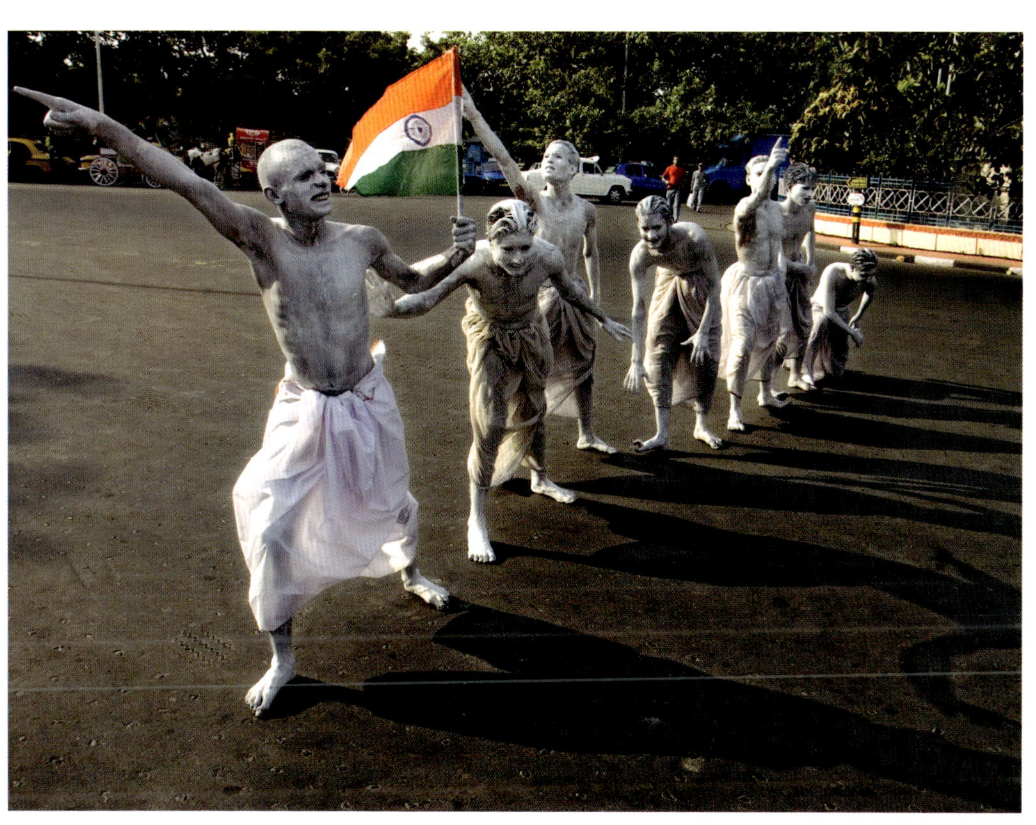

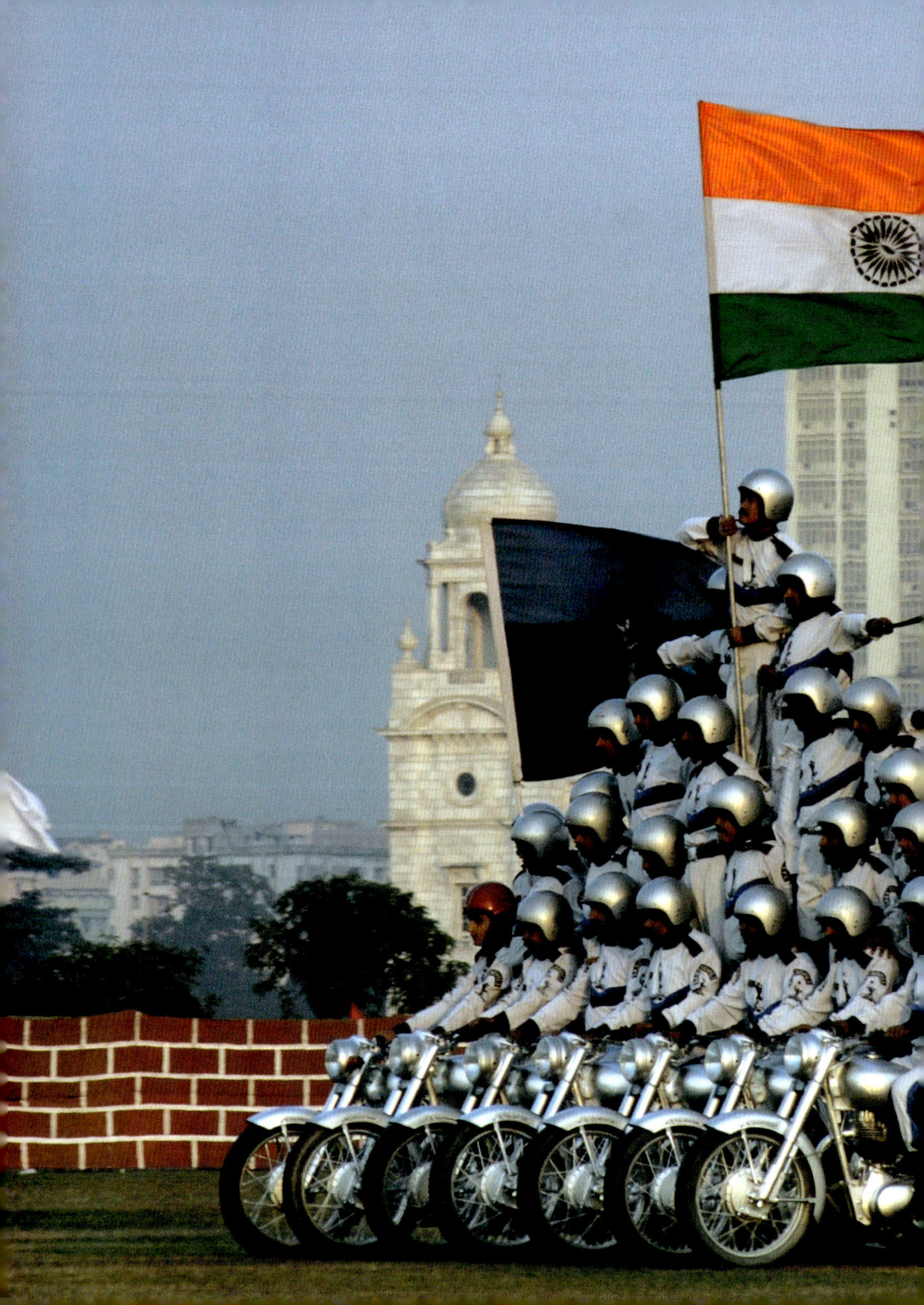

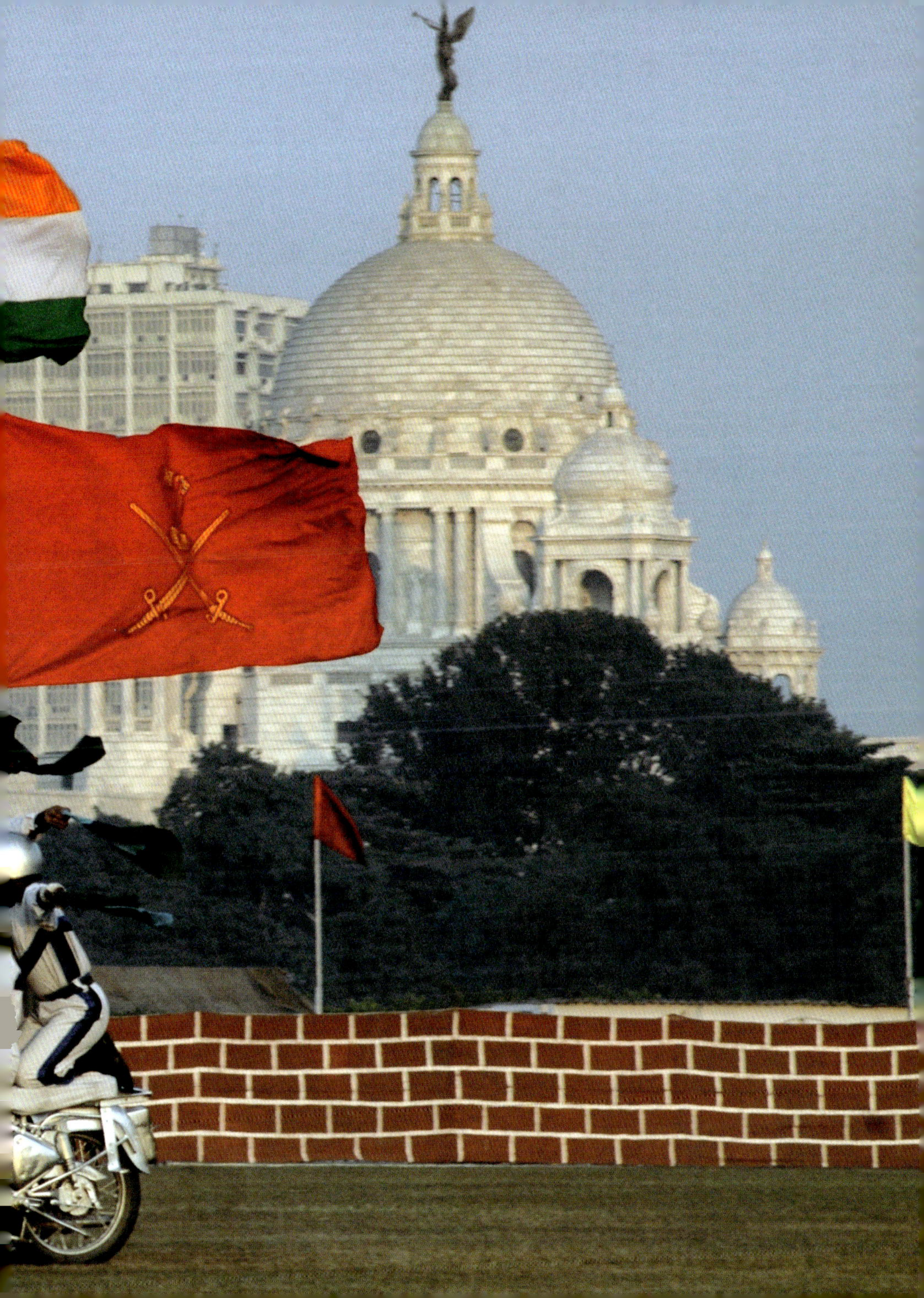

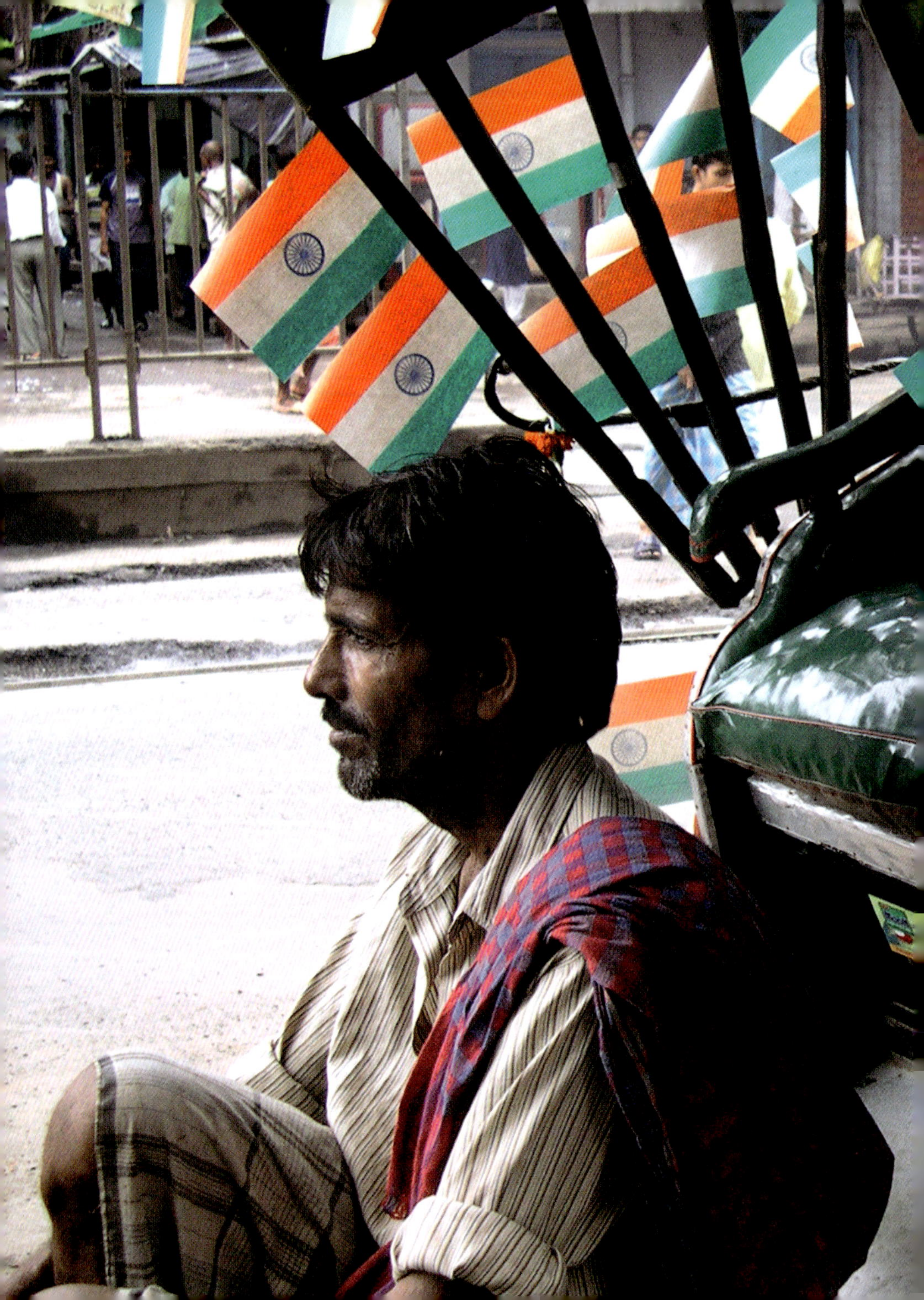

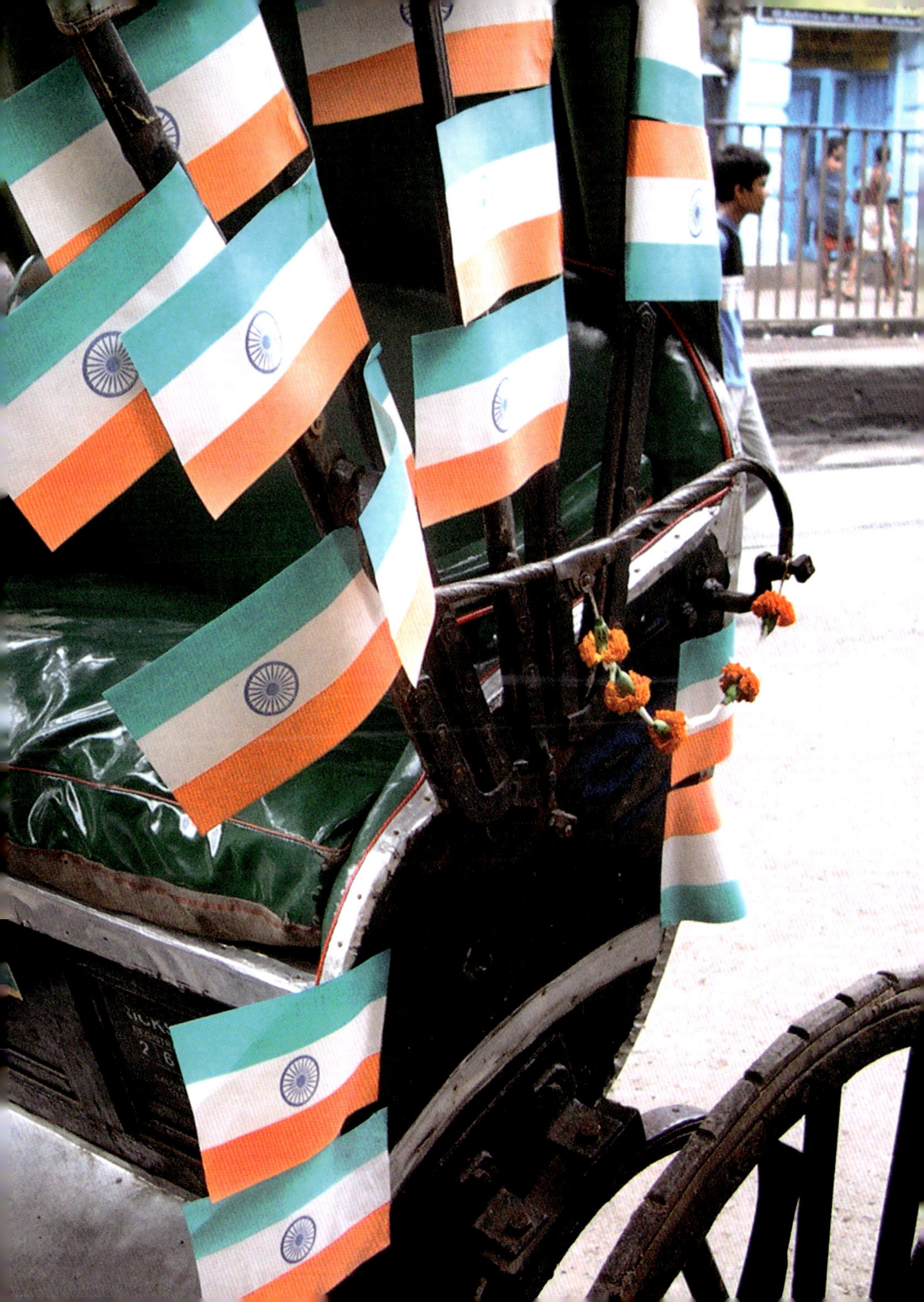

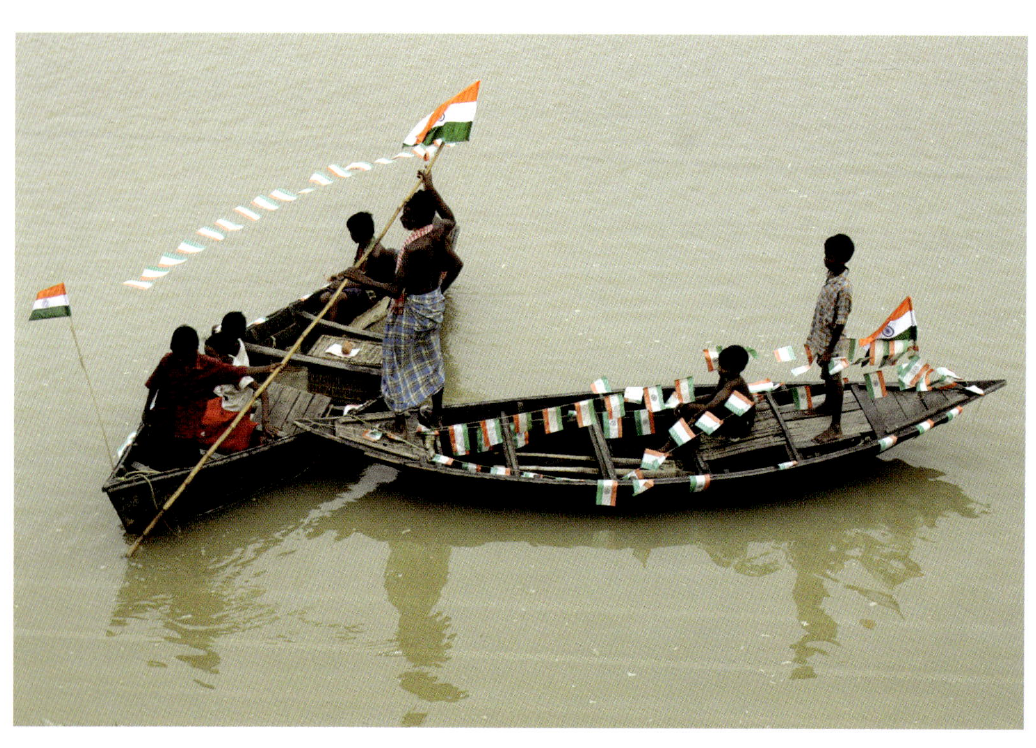

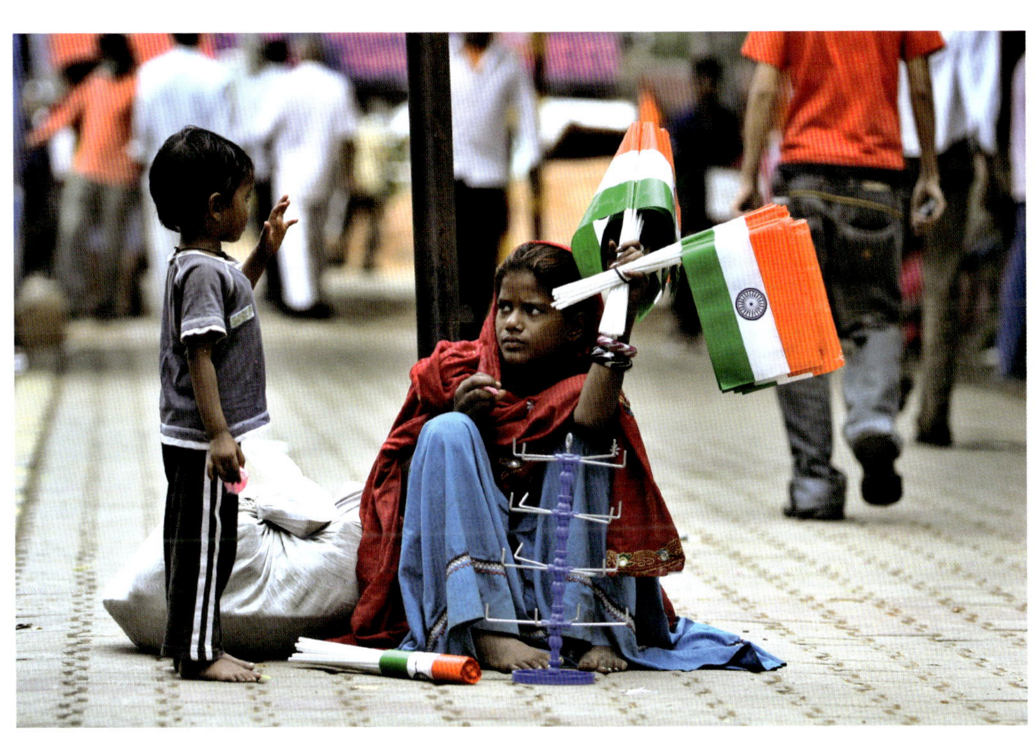

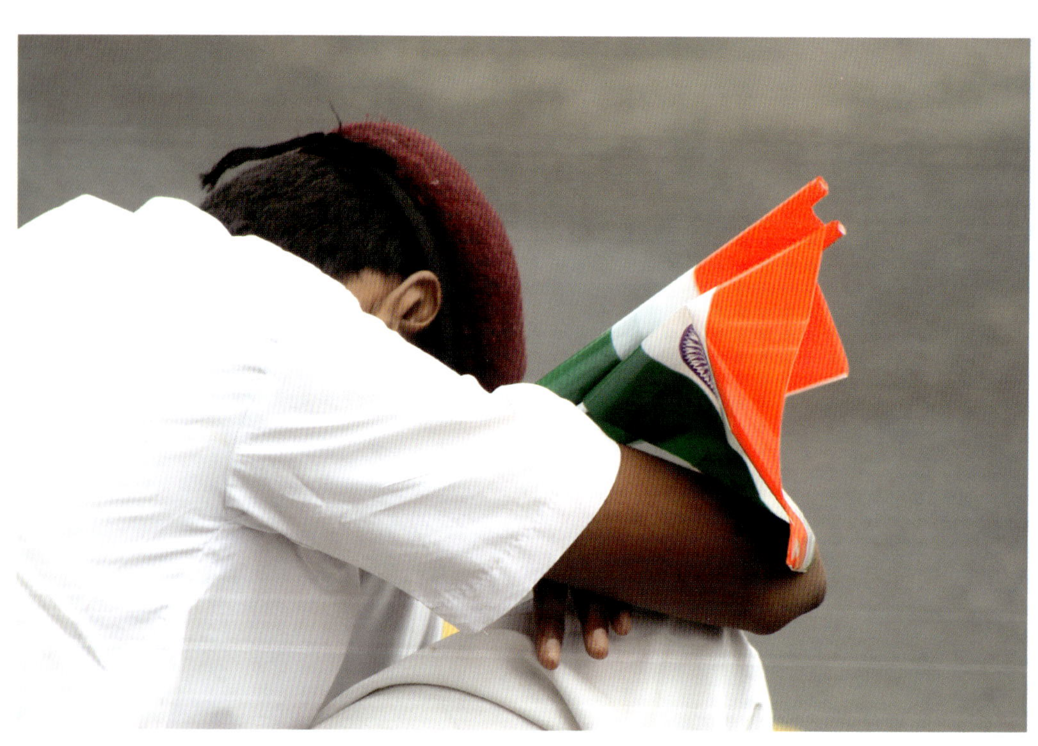

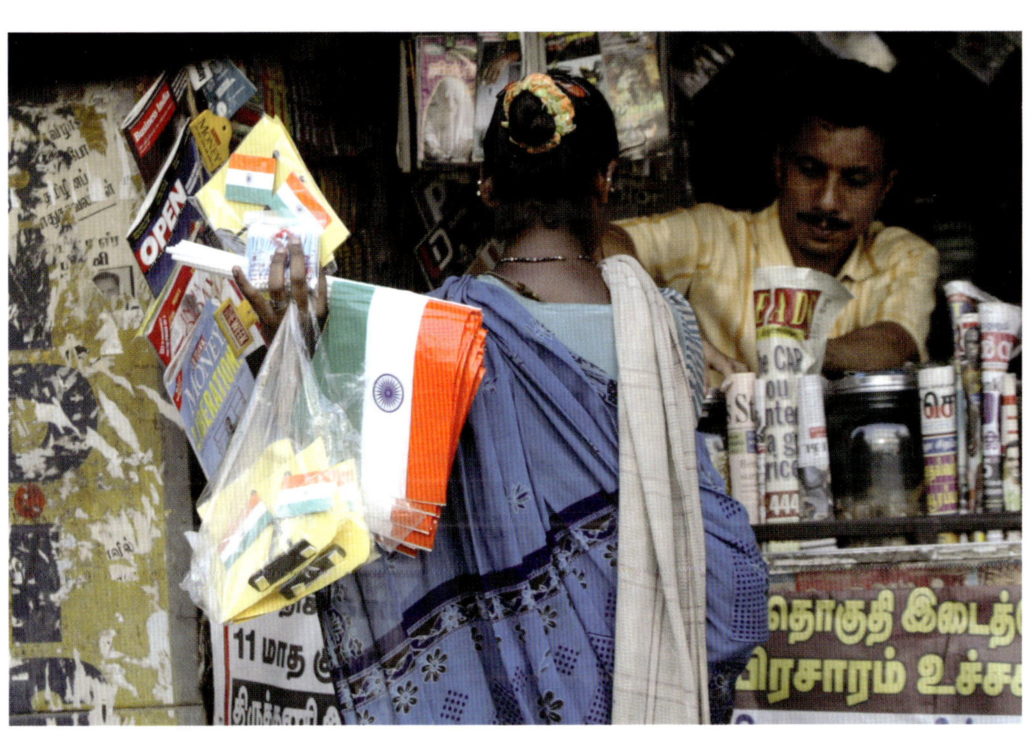

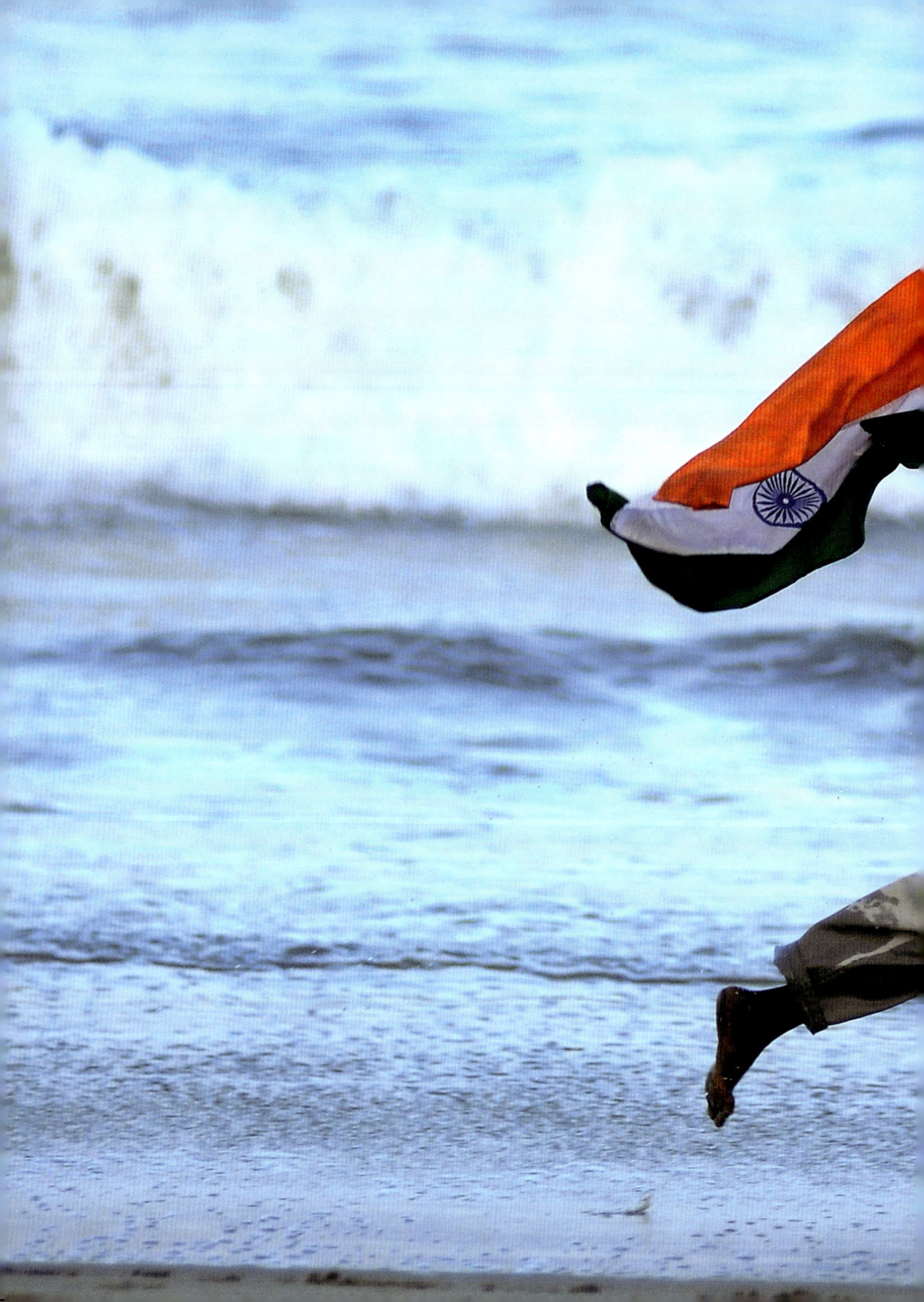

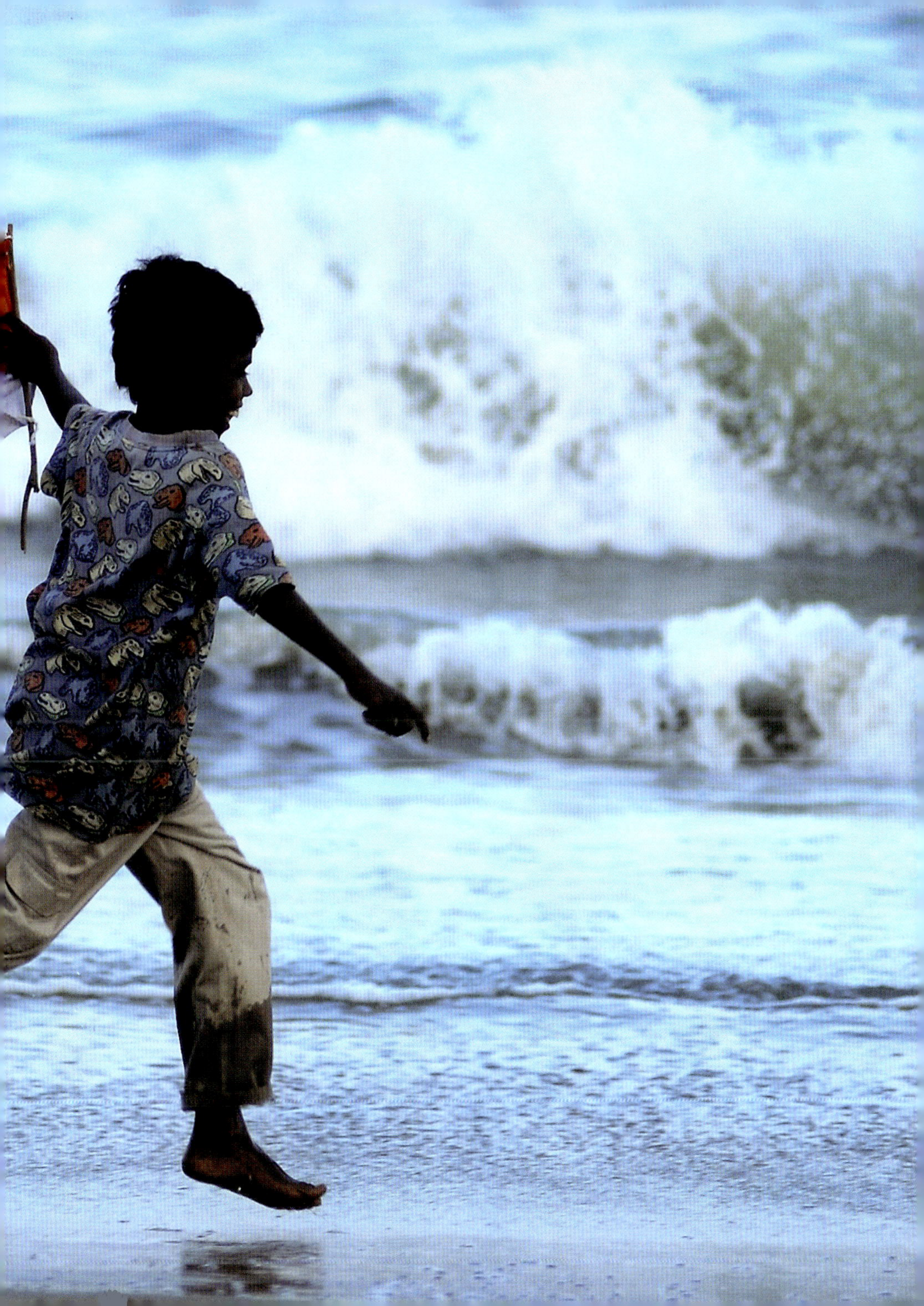

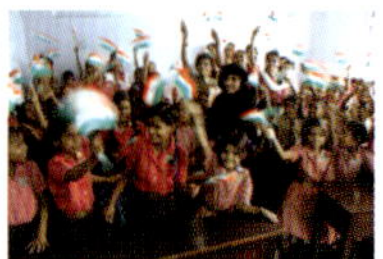

Supriya Biswas
Kolkata 2007

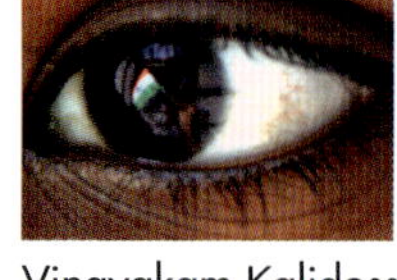

Vinayakam Kalidoss
Chennai 2008

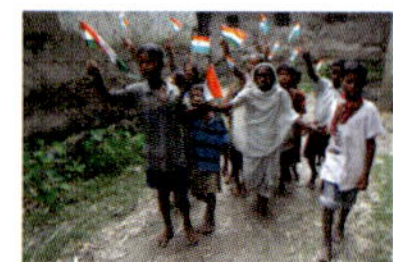

Supriya Biswas
Kolkata 2008

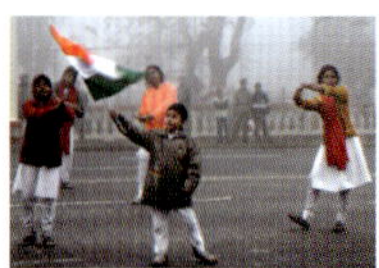

Chandan Dey
Kolkata 2009

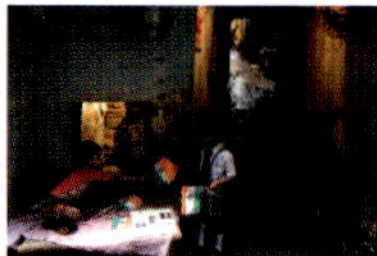

Sudipto Das
Varanasi 2008

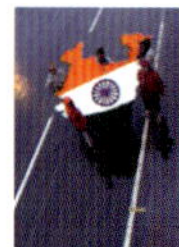

Supriya Biswas
Kolkata 2008

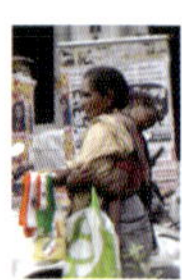

G. Murugan
Chennai 2008

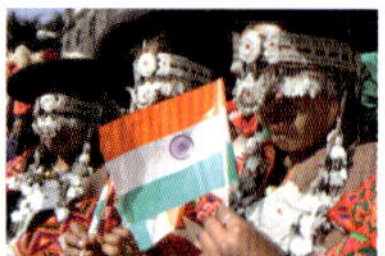

Anil Dayal
Shimla 2008

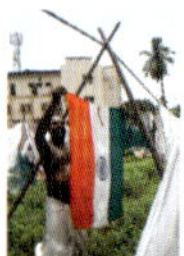

T. Mohandas
Kozhikode 2009

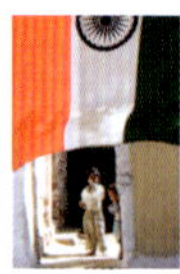

Prakash Hatvalne
Raipur 2006

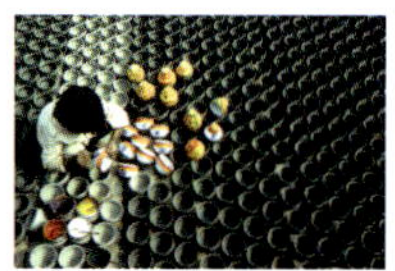

Supriya Biswas
Hooghly 2008

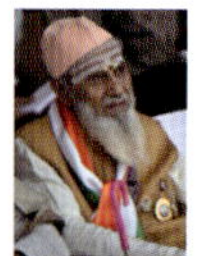

Nishant Ratnakar
Bengaluru 2009

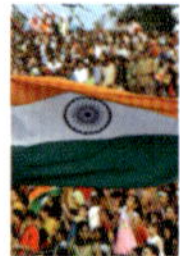

Shome Basu
Mumbai 2008

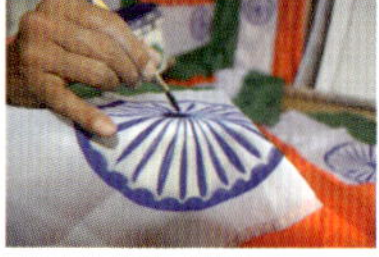

Arijit Saha
Brahmapur 2009

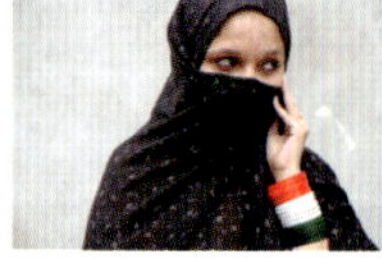

Pawan Kumar
Lucknow 2007

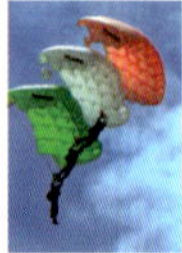

M. Lakshmanan
Chennai 2004

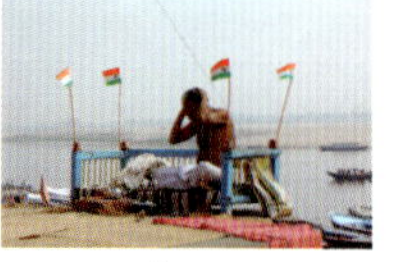

Arijit Saha
Varanasi 2008

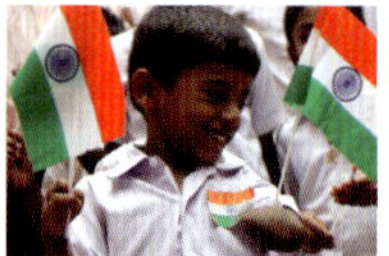

M. Srinivasan
Chennai 2008

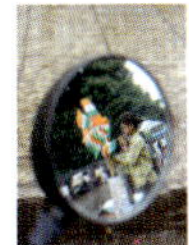

Raju Sanadi
Karad 2008

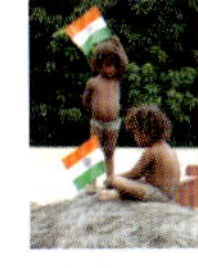

M. Srinivasan
Chennai 2005

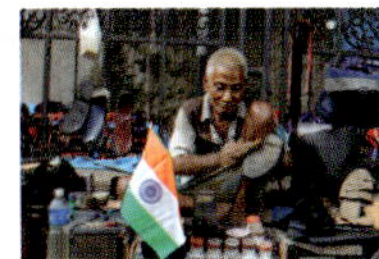

Arijit Saha
Kolkata 2007

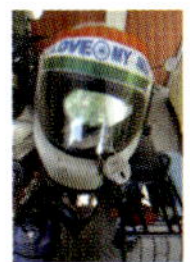

Vijaykumar
Chennai 2008

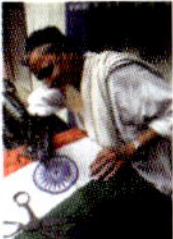

Supriya Biswas
Kolkata 2008

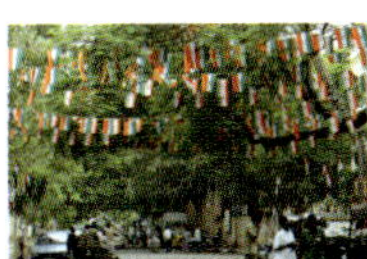

M. Lakshmanan
Chennai 2009

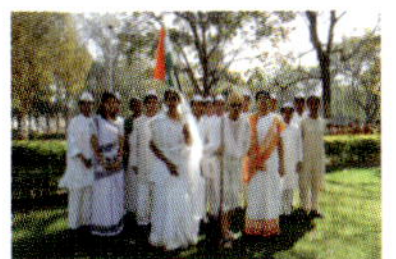

Raju Sanadi
Karad 2009

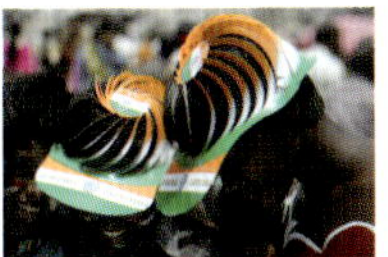

M. Lakshmanan
Chennai 2009

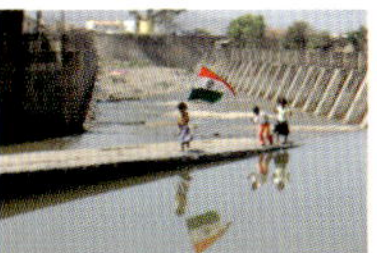

Raju Sanadi
Karad 2009

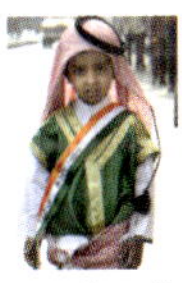

Piyal Adhikary
Kolkata 2006

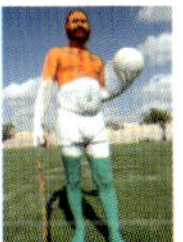

Dinesh Gupta
Bikaner 2007

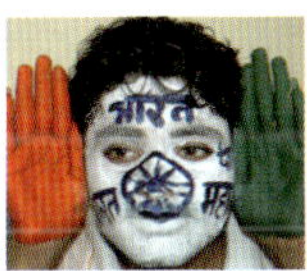

Dinesh Gupta
Bikaner 2008

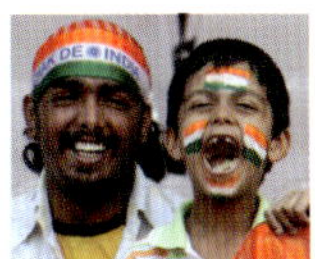

C. Ganesh
Chennai 2008

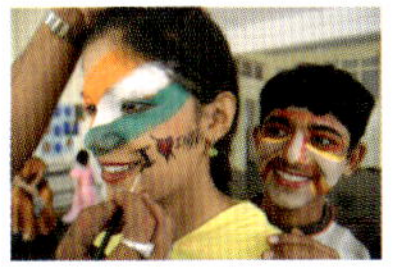

Kiran Bakale
Hubballi 2006

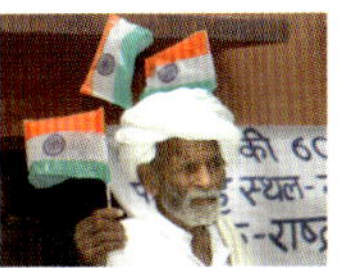

Dinesh Gupta
Bikaner 2007

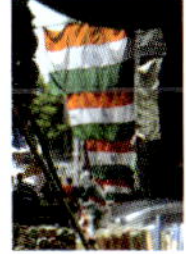

M. Lakshmanan
Chennai 2009

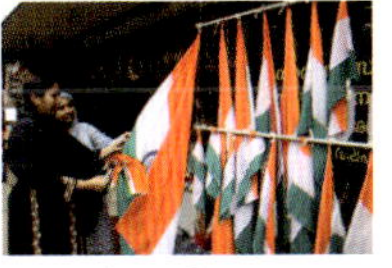

T. Mohandas
Kozhikode 2009

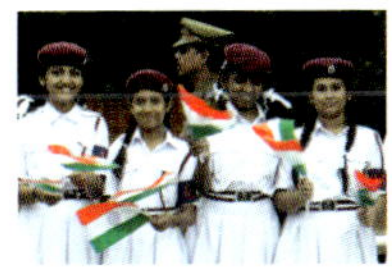

M. Lakshmanan
Chennai 2008

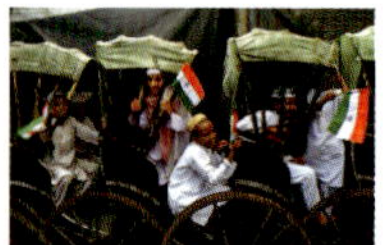

Supriya Biswas
Kolkata 2007

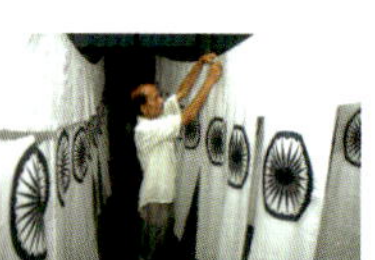

Manas Paran
Guwahati 2009

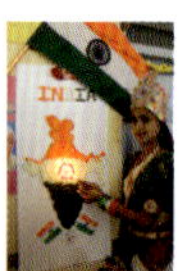

Kiran Bakale
Hubballi 2005

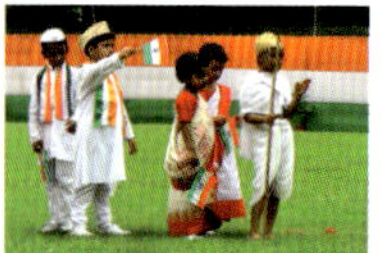

Shyamal Das
Murshidabad 2008

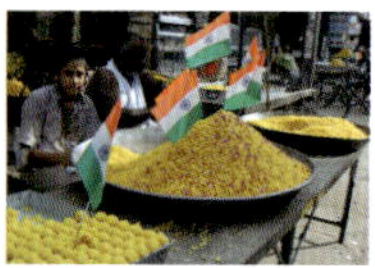

Dinesh Gupta
Bikaner 2008

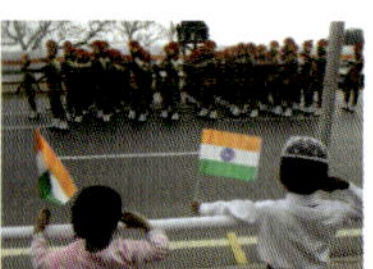

Piyal Adhikary
Kolkata 2006

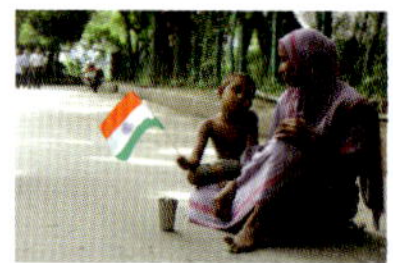

Arijit Saha
Kolkata 2007

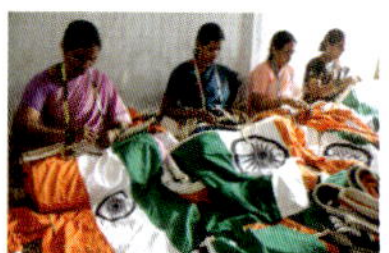

Kiran Bakale
Hubballi 2006

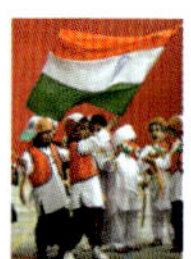

Anil Dayal
Shimla 2008

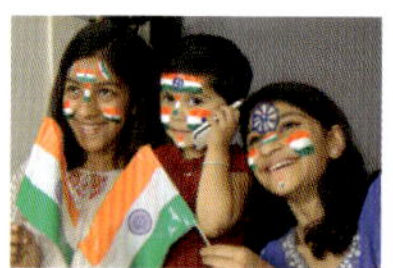

Kiran Bakale
Hubballi 2005

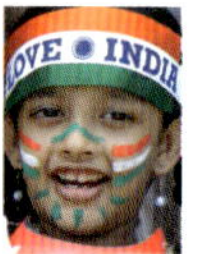

C. Ganesh
Chennai 2008

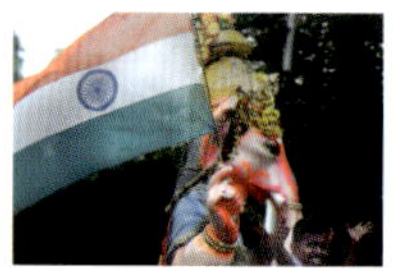

M. Lakshmanan
Chennai 2007

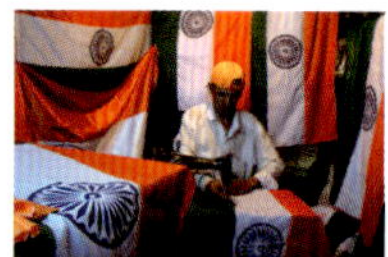

Surajit Roy
Manikpur, Malda 2008

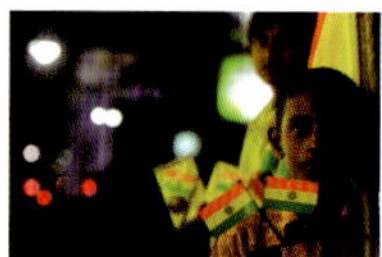

Selva Prakash
Bengaluru 2009

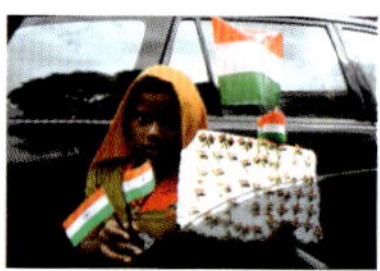

Selva Prakash
Bengaluru 2009

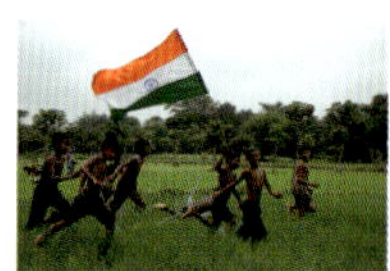

Surajit Roy
Manikpur, Malda 2008

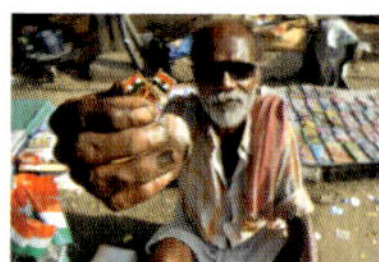

Nathan G.
Chennai 2009

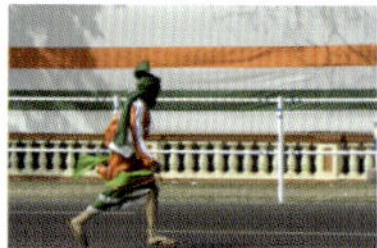

Aniruddha Pal
Kolkata 2009

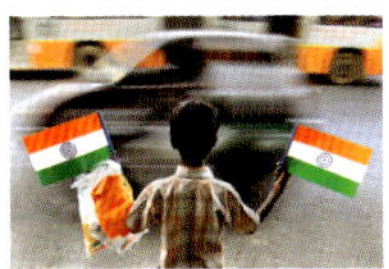

Nathan G.
Chennai 2009

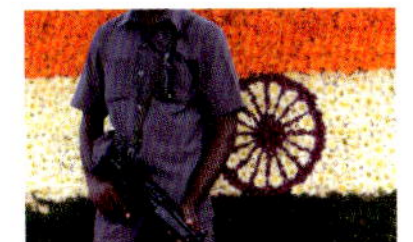

M. Lakshmanan
Chennai 2004

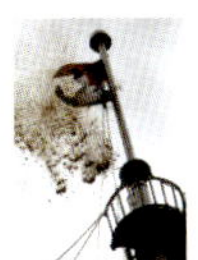

L. Palani
Chennai 2007

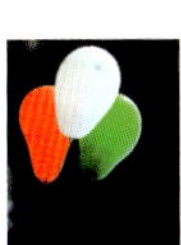

M. Lakshmanan
Chennai 2006

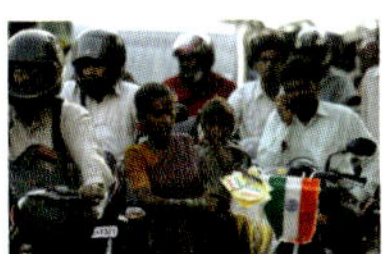

M. Lakshmanan
Chennai 2009

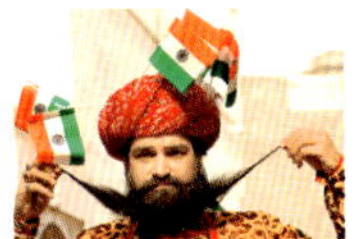

Dinesh Gupta
Bikaner 2008

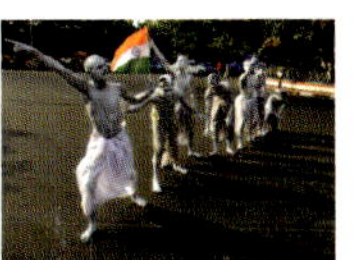

Sudipto Das
Kolkata 2007

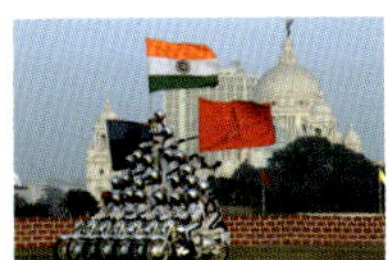

Sudipto Das
Kolkata 2005

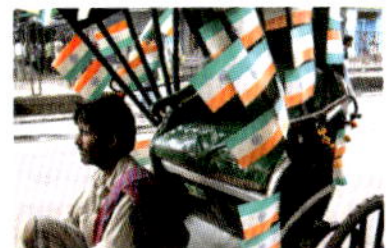

Sudipto Das
Kolkata 2007

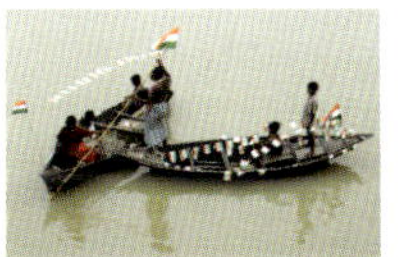

Aniruddha Pal
Balarampur, WB 2008

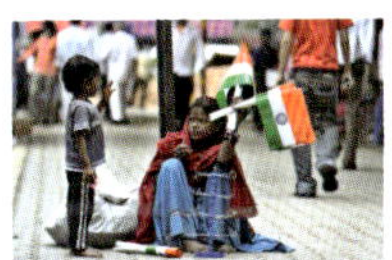

Nishant Ratnakar
Bengaluru 2009

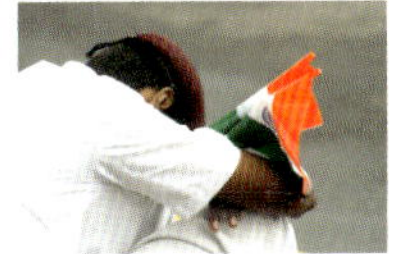

Paulraj Vijayan
Chennai 2009

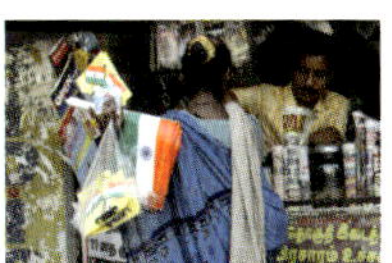

M. Lakshmanan
Chennai 2009

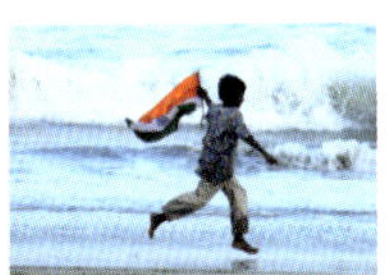

Shanthakumar
Chennai 2009

Former Deputy Photo Editor and Principal Photo Coordinator for the Press Trust of India, currently working for The Associated Press (AP), **M. Lakshmanan** is a seasoned photographer and winner of several national and international awards.

The Flag
Copyright © Tara Books Pvt. Ltd. 2010
For the photographs: individual artists
For this edition:
Tara Books Pvt. Ltd., India (www.tarabooks.com)
and Tara Publishing Ltd., UK (www.tarabooks.com/uk)

Edited by: M. Lakshmanan
Design: Jonathan Yamakami
Production: C. Arumugam
Printed at Asia Pacific Offset, China

ISBN 978-93-80340-05-0